D1462693

GOD'S LITTLE LESSONS FOR LEADERS

Honor Books
Tulsa, Oklahoma

God's Little Lessons for Leaders
ISBN 1-56292-996-8
Copyright © 2001 by Honor Books
P.O. Box 55388
Tulsa, Oklahoma 74155

INTRODUCTION

Leadership is an awesome responsibility. It requires vision, integrity, sensitivity, courage, sound judgment, and much more. Where can leaders find the resources they need to obtain these virtues?

God's Word is filled with the instruction and encouragement leaders need to face their most challenging responsibilities with confidence. It offers advice on topics as diverse as courage and character, faith and family, honesty and hope, work and worry. In fact, the Bible contains all the wisdom you will ever need to be a successful leader.

That's why we have included so much Scripture in this helpful little book. But *God's Little Lessons for Leaders* is more than a book of Bible verses. It also provides powerful devotional stories to help you live each day successfully. We pray that as you read through the pages of this special book, you will discover all that God has for you as a person and as a leader.

TABLE OF CONTENTS

ANGER

My beloved brethren, let every man be swift to hear, slow to speak, slow to wrath: For the wrath of man worketh not the righteousness of God.

James 1:19-20 KJV

A gentle answer turns away wrath, but a harsh word stirs up anger.

Proverbs 15:1

You yourselves are to put off all these: anger, wrath, malice, blasphemy, filthy language out of your mouth.

Colossians 3:8 NKJV

Cease from anger, and forsake wrath: fret not thyself in any wise to do evil.

Psalm 37:8 KJV

TRUE SUCCESS

Bobby Jones, one of golf's greatest players, was only five years old when he first swung a golf club. By the age of twelve, he was winning club tournaments. During this time, he was known for his hot temper, and he soon had the nickname "Club Thrower."

Jones became friends with a man named Grandpa Bart, who worked part-time in the club pro shop. Bart had been an excellent golfer but had retired when arthritis gripped his hands. After Bobby lost the National Amateur Tournament at the age of fourteen, he said, "Bobby, you are good enough to win that tournament, but you'll never win until you can control that temper of yours. You miss a shot—you get upset—then you lose."

Bobby knew Grandpa Bart was right, and he became determined to improve—not his golf swing—his mood swings. When Bobby won a major tournament at age twenty-one, Grandpa Bart said, "Bobby was fourteen when he mastered the game of golf, but he was twenty-one when he mastered himself."

Records are always established in relationship to other people's performance, but the true "standard of success" is established within the competitor. Let your "standard of success" be one that includes controlling your temper and taming your tongue. As a leader, you will be setting a Godly example for others to follow.

ANGER

An angry man stirs up strife, And a hot-tempered man abounds in transgression.

Proverbs 29:22 NASB

Do not associate with one easily angered, or you may learn his ways and get yourself ensnared.

Proverbs 22:24-25

10

He that is slow to anger is better than the mighty; and he that ruleth his spirit than he that taketh a city.

Proverbs 16:32 KJV

If you stay calm, you are wise, but if you have a hot temper, you only show how stupid you are.

Proverbs 14:29 TEV

MERE HABIT

General Horace Porter once wrote about a conversation he had with General Ulysses Grant one evening while they were sitting by a campfire. Porter noted, "General, it seems singular that you should have gone through all the rough and tumble of army service and frontier life and have never been provoked into swearing. I have never heard you utter an oath."

Grant replied, "Well, somehow or other, I never learned to swear. When I was a boy, I seemed to have an aversion to it, and when I became a man, I saw the folly of it. I have always noticed, too, that swearing helps to arouse a man's anger; and when a man flies into a passion, his adversary who keeps cool always gets the better of him. In fact, I could never see the value of swearing. I think it is the case with many people who swear excessively that it is a mere habit . . . they do not mean to be profane; to say the least, it is a great waste of time."

Not only does anger give rise to harsh words, but harsh words feed anger. The seething soul uses up valuable inner energy, leaving far less for the normal healthy functioning of the spirit, mind, and body. To rid yourself of feelings of anger and frustration, perhaps the first step is to watch your tongue!

ATTITUDE

As he thinks in his heart, so is he.

Proverbs 23:7 NKJV

A merry heart doeth good like a medicine: but a broken spirit drieth the bones.

Proverbs 17:22 KJV

12   Happy are those who fear the LORD. Yes, happy are those who delight in doing what he commands.

Psalm 112:1 NLT

When people are happy, they smile, but when they are sad, they look depressed.

Proverbs 15:13 TEV

LIGHTEN UP

T he great preacher Charles H. Spurgeon once emphasized to a preaching class that a speaker's facial expressions should harmonize with the sermon. He suggested that "when you speak of Heaven, let your face light up, let it be irradiated with a heavenly gleam, let your eyes shine with reflected glory. But when you speak of hell, well, then your ordinary face will do."

While we may think it fake to "force" an attitude of cheerfulness or a facial expression, such as a smile, scientific documentation has proved that sustaining a cheerful expression actually uses less muscle power than maintaining a frown. Researchers also note that an optimistic, upbeat attitude can more easily defuse pressure and stress than an attitude of pessimism. And medical science has long recognized the profound, instantaneous benefits of laughter on virtually every important organ in the human body. Even forced laughter reduces health-sapping tension while it simultaneously relaxes the muscles and exercises the organs. In fact, three minutes of sustained laughter will exercise your body as much as thirty minutes on a rowing machine.

Lighten up your outlook to relieve nervousness, tension, or fatigue. Indulge in a daily dose of laughter, and discover its beneficial effects, both mentally and physically.

ATTITUDE

[Jesus] said to them, " . . . Truly I say to you, if you have faith the size of a mustard seed, you shall say to this mountain, 'Move from here to there,' and it will move; and nothing will be impossible to you."

Matthew 17:20 NASB

14

Faith comes by hearing, and hearing by the word of God.

Romans 10:17 NKJV

The boy's father exclaimed, "I do believe; help me overcome my unbelief!"

Mark 9:24

To have faith is to be sure of the things we hope for, to be certain of the things we cannot see.

Hebrews 11:1 TEV

AWFUL ATTITUDE

Cheryl continually complained that she didn't make enough money, couldn't afford the things she wanted, and therefore, wasn't ever going to amount to anything. A counselor said to her, "You're throwing your energy away complaining instead of using it to get ahead."

"But you don't understand, I'm not the problem," Cheryl countered.

The counselor said, "Your low-paying job may be a problem, and your boss may demand too much, but if you are continually that upset, you are causing yourself more harm than either the job or the boss."

"What can I do?" she asked.

The counselor said, "You can't control your boss or the job, but you can control how you *feel* about them. Change your attitude."

Cheryl took her advice. When she stopped whining about her life, people around her noticed. She got a promotion, and with her new job status, she was more marketable. Within several months, she was transferred out of the department into a position with even higher pay and a more supportive boss.

Awful is a state of *attitude*. A wise leader realizes that a change in attitude will change the state of things!

CHARACTER

Do not be misled: "Bad company corrupts good character."

1 Corinthians 15:33

We also rejoice in our sufferings, because we know that suffering produces perseverance; perseverance, character; and character, hope.

Romans 5:3-4

A wife of noble character who can find? She is worth far more than rubies.

Proverbs 31:10

Dear brothers, you have no obligations whatever to your old sinful nature to do what it begs you to do. For if you keep on following it you are lost and will perish, but if through the power of the Holy Spirit you crush it and its evil deeds, you shall live.

Romans 8:12-13 TLB

16

TRUE CHARACTER

The following set of contrasting remarks has been offered as a character sketch of a good leader. For a personal challenge, as you read through the list, circle the descriptive words you believe most closely identify *you!*

- Self-reliant but not Self-sufficient
- Energetic but not Self-seeking
- Steadfast but not Stubborn
- Tactful but not Timid
- Serious but not Sullen
- Loyal but not Sectarian
- Unmovable but not Stationary
- Gentle but not Hypersensitive
- Tenderhearted but not Touchy
- Conscientious but not a Perfectionist
- Disciplined but not Demanding
- Generous but not Gullible
- Meek but not Weak
- Humorous but not Hilarious
- Friendly but not Familiar
- Holy but not Holier-than-thou
- Discerning but not Critical
- Progressive but not Pretentious
- Authoritative but not Autocratic

Now, ask God to help you develop the character traits described in the words you didn't circle.

CONFLICT

How good and pleasant it is when brothers live together in unity!

Psalm 133:1

May the God of steadfastness and encouragement grant you to live in such harmony with one another, in accord with Christ Jesus, that together you may with one voice glorify the God and Father of our Lord Jesus Christ.

Romans 15:5-6 RSV

Try always to be led along together by the Holy Spirit, and so be at peace with one another.

Ephesians 4:3 TLB

Don't grumble about each other, brothers. Are you yourselves above criticism? For see! The great Judge is coming.

James 5:9 TLB

THE <u>TONDELAYO</u>

In *The Fall of Fortresses,* Elmer Bendiner tells of a miracle that happened to him and a few others aboard their B-17 bomber, the *Tondelayo.* During a run over Kassel, Germany, the plane was barraged by Nazi antiaircraft guns. That in itself was not unusual, but on this particular flight the fuel tanks of the plane were hit. The following morning, the pilot Bohn Fawkes asked the crew chief for the shell as a souvenir of their unbelievable luck.

Bohn was then told that not just one shell had been found in the gas tanks, but eleven!

The shells were sent to the armorers to be defused. Later they informed the *Tondelayo* crew that when they opened the shells, they found no explosive charge in any of them. One of the shells, however, contained a carefully rolled piece of paper. On it was scrawled in the Czech language: "This is all we can do for you now." The miracle had not been one of misfired shells, but of peace-loving hearts.

If you want peace in your life, you first must disarm your weapons—your painful words, prideful looks, and hurtful attitudes. As a leader, it is important to diffuse conflict in favor of unity; then God will flood your life with His peace and love.

CONFUSION

If you want to know what God wants you to do, ask him, and he will gladly tell you, for he is always ready to give a bountiful supply of wisdom to all who ask him; he will not resent it.

James 1:5 TLB

God is not the author of confusion, but of peace.

1 Corinthians 14:33 KJV

The LORD will accomplish what concerns me;
Your lovingkindness, O LORD, is everlasting.

Psalm 138:8 NASB

Call to Me, and I will answer you, and show you great and mighty things, which you do not know.

Jeremiah 33:3 NKJV

20

JUST ONE TREE

A young man was concerned about the uncertainty of his future and confused about which direction to take with his life. He sat quietly on a park bench, watching squirrels scamper among the trees. Suddenly, a squirrel jumped from one high tree to another, aiming for a limb so far out of reach that the leap looked like sheer suicide. Though the squirrel missed its mark, it landed safely and seemingly unconcerned on a branch several feet below. The squirrel then scampered upward to its original goal, and all was well.

An old man was sitting on the other end of the bench. "Funny thing," the man remarked. "I've seen hundreds of 'em jump like that. A lot of 'em miss, but I've never seen any hurt in trying." Then the man chuckled and added, "I guess they've got to risk something if they don't want to spend their lives in just one tree."

The young man thought, *A squirrel takes a chance—have I less nerve than a squirrel?* He made up his mind in that moment to take the risk he had been considering, and sure enough, he landed safer and higher than he had dared to imagine.

Break through confusion by taking a bold leap of faith!

COURAGE

Don't be afraid, for I am with you. Do not be
dismayed, for I am your God. I will strengthen
you. I will help you. I will uphold you with my
victorious right hand.

Isaiah 41:10 NLT

22

Be strong and let your heart take courage,
All you who hope in the LORD.

Psalm 31:24 NASB

Be on your guard; stand firm in the faith; be men
of courage; be strong.

1 Corinthians 16:13

The fear of man brings a snare,
But whoever trusts in the LORD shall be safe.

Proverbs 29:25 NKJV

FIGHTIN' WORDS

Perhaps more than any other leader in the twentieth century, Winston Churchill rallied a nation to believe in what it *could* do. His speeches during World War II not only expressed resolution, but also a profound peace of mind and a feeling of "rightness." Here are some of his inspiring words to England and the world:

You ask, "What is our policy?" I will say: It is to wage war, by sea, land, and air, with all our might and all the strength that God can give us. . . . You ask, "What is our aim?" I can answer in one word: Victory . . . at all costs, victory in spite of all terror, victory however long and hard the road may be; for without victory there is no survival. . . . We shall go on to the end, we shall fight in France, we shall fight on the seas and oceans, we shall fight with growing confidence and growing strength in the air, we shall defend our island, whatever the cost may be; we shall fight on the beaches, we shall fight on the landing grounds, we shall fight in the fields and in the streets, we shall fight in the hills; we shall never surrender.

What wonderful words to adapt to any fight against evil!

COURAGE

That he would grant unto us, that we being delivered out of the hand of our enemies might serve him without fear.

Luke 1:74 KJV

Be strong and courageous. . . . the LORD your God goes with you; he will never leave you nor forsake you.

Deuteronomy 31:6

Christ gives me the strength to face anything.

Philippians 4:13 CEV

We say with confidence, "The Lord is my helper; I will not be afraid. What can man do to me?"

Hebrews 13:6

24

THE RIGHT THING

Illinois is considered one of the most prosperous states in the nation today. Many regard an action taken by Stephen Douglas as the origin of that prosperity.

The nation was undergoing a financial depression in the mid-1800s, and state governments began to panic about their potential financial losses. Pennsylvania refused to pay its debts although it was considered a rich state at the time. Illinois, a poor state at that time, felt justified that it might also take this route in confronting its debt.

When Stephen Douglas heard of this possibility, he opposed the idea with all his might. Although he was seriously ill, he insisted that he be carried on a stretcher to his place in the state legislature. Lying on his back, he made a historic resolution: "That Illinois be honest." His motion touched the deepest sense of morality in every member of the legislature. It was overwhelmingly adopted. The practice of repudiation was dealt a deathblow. The result was that Illinois had to find a new way out of its financial slump—a way that turned out to be one of investment, growth, and eventually, prosperity.

Doing the right thing always pays off—usually not right away, but the momentary relief of an easy solution is nothing compared with the eternal joy of choosing right.

DEPRESSION

In my great trouble I cried to the Lord and he
answered me; from the depths of death I called,
and Lord, you heard me!

Jonah 2:2 TLB

Answer me quickly, O LORD; my spirit fails. Do not
hide your face from me or I will be like those who
go down to the pit. Let the morning bring me
word of your unfailing love, for I have put my trust
in you. Show me the way I should go, for to you I
lift up my soul.

Psalm 143:7-8

I will refresh the weary and satisfy the faint.

Jeremiah 31:25

The LORD also will be a refuge for the oppressed,
A refuge in times of trouble.

Psalm 9:9 NKJV

OVERCOMERS

In 1980, Mount Saint Helens erupted, and the Pacific Northwest shuddered under its devastating impact. Forests were destroyed by fire. Rivers were choked with debris. Fish and other wildlife died. Toxic fumes filled the air, and reporters ominously predicted that acid rain would develop from the ash-laden clouds. The future for the area seemed bleak.

Nevertheless, less than a year after the eruption, scientists discovered that despite the fact that the rivers had been clogged with hot mud, volcanic ash, and floating debris, some of the salmon and steelhead had managed to survive. By using alternate streams and waterways, some of which were less than six inches deep, the fish returned home to spawn.

Within a few short years, the fields, lakes, and rivers surrounding Mount Saint Helens teemed with life. The water and soil seemed to benefit from the nutrients supplied by the exploding volcano. Even the mountain itself began to show signs of new vegetation.

Challenges in life can enrich you and make you stronger. Trouble may only be the means to show you a different way to go, a different way to lead. It may be an opportunity to start afresh. Regardless of the challenges you face, always remember that you are God's creation, and you were designed to overcome!

DEPRESSION

We have troubles all around us, but we are not defeated. We do not know what to do, but we do not give up the hope of living. We are persecuted, but God does not leave us. We are hurt sometimes, but we are not destroyed.

2 Corinthians 4:8-9 NCV

Cast your burden upon the LORD and He will sustain you; He will never allow the righteous to be shaken.

Psalm 55:22 NASB

God is our refuge and strength, a tested help in times of trouble.

Psalm 46:1 TLB

[Jesus said]: "In this world you will have trouble. But take heart! I have overcome the world."

John 16:33

THE FOG OF DEPRESSION

On a cool morning in July of 1952, Florence Chadwick waded into the waters off of Catalina Island, intending to swim the channel to the California coast. Though an experienced long-distance swimmer, Florence knew this swim would be difficult. The water was numbingly cold, and the fog was so thick she could hardly see the boat that carried her trainer.

Florence swam for more than fifteen hours. Several times she could sense sharks swimming next to her in the inky waters. Rifles were fired from the trainer's boat to help keep the sharks at bay. Yet when Florence looked around her, all she could see was the fog. When she finally asked to be lifted from the water, she was only a half-mile from her goal. In a later interview, Florence admitted that it wasn't the cold, fear, or exhaustion that caused her to fail in her attempt to swim the Catalina Channel. It was the fog.

The struggles we face can sometimes cloak us in a fog of depression. Remember, even if you can't see the end of your trouble, press on. God hasn't brought you this far to leave you. He is standing there just outside the fog, waiting for your call.

DISCOURAGEMENT

My mouth would encourage you; comfort from my lips would bring you relief.

Job 16:5

You are my hiding place from every storm of life; you even keep me from getting into trouble! You surround me with songs of victory.

Psalm 32:7 TLB

30

Those who know you, LORD, will trust you; you do not abandon anyone who comes to you.

Psalm 9:10 TEV

When life is good, enjoy it. But when life is hard, remember: God gives good times and hard times.

Ecclesiastes 7:14 NCV

YOU MUSTN'T QUIT

When things go wrong, as they sometimes will,
When the road you're trudging seems all uphill,
When the funds are low and the debts are high
And you want to smile, but you have to sigh,
When care is pressing you down a bit,
Rest! If you must—but never quit.
Life is queer, with its twists and turns,
As every one of us sometimes learns,
And many a failure turns about
When he might have won if he'd stuck it out;
Stick to your task, though the pace seems slow.
You may succeed with one more blow.
Success is failure turned inside out,
The silver tint of the clouds of doubt.
And you never can tell how close you are,
It may be near when it seems afar;
So stick to the fight when you're hardest hit.
It's when things seem worst that
YOU MUSTN'T QUIT.

—Unknown

DISCOURAGEMENT

We gladly suffer, because we know that suffering helps us to endure. And endurance builds character, which gives us a hope that will never disappoint us. All of this happens because God has given us the Holy Spirit, who fills our hearts with his love.

Romans 5:3-5 CEV

32

[Love] always protects, always trusts, always hopes, always perseveres.

1 Corinthians 13:7

Blessed is the man who endures trial, for when he has stood the test he will receive the crown of life which God has promised to those who love him.

James 1:12 RSV

May the Lord direct your hearts into God's love and Christ's perseverance.

2 Thessalonians 3:5

ONE MORE ROUND

Prizefighter James J. Corbett made many memorable statements during his colorful career, but perhaps his most famous was when he was asked, "What is the most important thing for a man to do to become a champion?" Corbett replied, "Fight one more round."

Many successful people have had that perspective. Thomas Gray wrote seventy-five drafts of "Elegy Written in a Country Churchyard" before he was satisfied with his poetic masterpiece. S. N. Behrman, an American playwright, wrote plays for eleven years before he sold one. Somerset Maugham earned only $500 in his first ten years as a writer. While working full-time in a factory, Enrico Caruso studied voice for twelve years before he became a successful performer. George Gershwin composed almost one hundred melodies before he sold his first one—for $5.00. During his first five years as a writer, Zane Grey couldn't sell a single story.

Don't be discouraged if your dream doesn't come true immediately. Continue to pursue your craft or talent. Study and learn. Grow by experience. Keep working. The victory goes to those who are willing to fight "one more round"!

ENCOURAGEMENT

The righteous face many troubles, but the LORD rescues them from each and every one.

Psalm 34:19 NLT

The Lord says, "If you love me and truly know who I am, I will rescue you and keep you safe. When you are in trouble, call out to me. I will answer and be there to protect and honor you."

Psalm 91:14-15 CEV

"These things I have spoken unto you, that in me ye might have peace. In the world ye shall have tribulation: but be of good cheer; I have overcome the world."

John 16:33 KJV

Humble yourselves therefore under the mighty hand of God, that in due time he may exalt you. Cast all your anxieties on him, for he cares about you.

1 Peter 5:6-7 RSV

AN ACT OF CONGRESS

Irwin, a junior naval officer, was discharged from military service after he was diagnosed with cancer—standard military procedure at the time. The loss of his job was quite a blow, but he was determined to get back both his health and his job. With faith and dogged determination, he battled the disease that tried to take over his body. At one point, he was given only two weeks to live, but eventually, his cancer was brought under control.

Irwin then focused his attention on his desire to become a naval officer. He discovered, however, that regulations forbade reinstatement of a person discharged with cancer. Everyone told Irwin, "Give up. It would take an act of Congress to get reinstated." Their advice gave him an idea—he would pursue an act of Congress!

President Harry S Truman eventually signed into law a special bill that allowed Irwin W. Rosenberg to reenlist and become a rear admiral in the United States Seventh Fleet!

The thought, "Where there's a will, there's a way" is applicable to nearly every circumstance in life. When your will lines up with God's will, He will help you accomplish your dream!

ENCOURAGEMENT

God's love, though, is ever and always, eternally present to all who fear him, Making everything right for them and their children as they follow his Covenant ways and remember to do whatever he said.

Psalm 103:17-18
THE MESSAGE

36

Trust in the Lord instead. Be kind and good to others; then you will live safely here in the land and prosper, feeding in safety. Be delighted with the Lord. Then he will give you all your heart's desires.

Psalm 37:3-4 TLB

The humble will see their God at work and be glad. Let all who seek God's help live in joy.

Psalm 69:32 NLT

Exhort one another daily, while it is called *"Today,"* lest any of you be hardened through the deceitfulness of sin.

Hebrews 3:13 NKJV

WORST TEAM IN THE NFL

ack-to-back victories by the Dallas Cowboys at the Super Bowl in 1993 and 1994 mask the fact that Jimmy Johnson, the team's legendary former coach, knew as much about losing as he did about winning. In 1989, his first season in Dallas, Johnson's team had only one win and fifteen losses! However, this overwhelming losing season was still not as humiliating as his first year as a high-school defensive coach, when his team finished the season with no wins and ten losses.

Johnson said about that first season in Dallas, "We had the worst team in the NFL, but I wouldn't accept anything but being in the Super Bowl."

Johnson kept a positive attitude. If a running back had the ball, he shouted, "Protect the ball," rather than "Don't fumble." To his field-goal kickers he'd say, "Make this," not "Don't miss." After a loss, he'd spend his post-game time plotting the next win, rather than second-guessing what had gone wrong.

The Cowboys responded and improved. It took four seasons of hard work, but then Super Bowl rings were on their fingers.[1]

You may not win every contest you pursue, but the person who plays to win always has a much better chance!

EXAMPLE

"I have set you an example that you should do as I have done for you."

John 13:15

Command and teach these things. Don't let anyone look down on you because you are young, but set an example for the believers in speech, in life, in love, in faith and in purity.

1 Timothy 4:11-12

38

If you suffer for doing good and you endure it, this is commendable before God. To this you were called, because Christ suffered for you, leaving you an example, that you should follow in his steps.

1 Peter 2:20-21

These things occurred as examples to keep us from setting our hearts on evil things.

1 Corinthians 10:6

THE UGLIEST MAN

President Lincoln had a disarming and engaging ability to laugh at himself, especially his own physical appearance. When Senator Stephen A. Douglas once called him a "two-faced man," Lincoln responded, "I leave it to my audience. If I had another face, do you think I would wear this one?"

Another time he told a group of editors about meeting a woman riding on horseback in the wood. "She looked at me intently and said, 'I do believe you are the ugliest man I ever saw.' Said I, 'Madam, you are probably right, but I can't help it.' 'No,' she said, 'you can't help it, but you might stay at home.'"

Although his likeness is widely recognized, Lincoln is not known primarily for his appearance but for his courageous stance for restoration of the Union and the abolition of slavery. He is often held up as an example of remarkable patience, determination, dedication, strong will, compassion, thoughtfulness, and selflessness. These inner qualities are what mark Lincoln as one of America's greatest presidents.

So much is made in our culture today of outward appearance and material possessions. Remember that it is your virtuous inner qualities that create a lasting reputation.

FAILURE

I am very happy to brag about my weaknesses.
Then Christ's power can live in me.
2 Corinthians 12:9 NCV

Our High Priest is not one who cannot feel
sympathy for our weaknesses. . . . Let us have
confidence, then, and approach God's throne,
where there is grace. There we will receive mercy
and find grace to help us just when we need it.
Hebrews 4:15-16 TEV

If we believe not, yet he abideth faithful: he
cannot deny himself.
2 Timothy 2:13 KJV

Plans go wrong for lack of advice; many
counselors bring success.
Proverbs 15:22 NLT

40

REFUSING TO FAIL

From an early age, Larry lived and breathed the sport of golf. As a teenager, he was ranked one of the top sixteen young golfers in the nation. Then at the beginning of his senior year of high school, Larry was in an automobile accident. He suffered severe injuries, but the most devastating was that his left arm had to be amputated just below the elbow.

Larry had never heard of a one-armed golfer, but then again, he didn't know that it couldn't be done! As Larry began to swing a few golf clubs at the rehab center, his mother and a psychologist sought out someone who could design a prosthetic hand for him. After several months of practice with his new hand, Larry hit a ball one day. When it landed more than 200 yards away, he knew he was "back." He rejoined his high-school team, scoring even better than before, and is now in college on a golf scholarship!

"Don't think of your missing limb as something that makes you a lesser person," Larry once told an audience of children who had lost limbs. "Think of it as something that can make you stronger. I would love to be the first pro golfer with a prosthetic hand. But I also know that if I don't succeed, I won't be a failure. We only fail if we don't try."

You may not always succeed at everything you do, but when you are confronted with obstacles, keep trying. Remember that God is always with you, and refuse to quit!

FAILURE

At least there is hope for a tree: If it is cut down, it
will sprout again, and its new shoots will not fail.
Its roots may grow old in the ground and its stump
die in the soil, yet at the scent of water it will bud
and put forth shoots like a plant.
Job 14:7-9

42

The Lord said, "Simon, Simon, behold, Satan hath
desired to have you, that he may sift you as wheat:
But I have prayed for thee, that thy faith
fail not: and when thou art converted, strengthen
thy brethren."
Luke 22:31-32 KJV

We can rejoice, too, when we run into problems
and trials, for we know that they are good for us—
they help us learn to endure. And endurance
develops strength of character in us, and character
strengthens our confident expectation of salvation.
Romans 5:3-4 NLT

We never give up. Our bodies are gradually dying,
but we ourselves are being made stronger each day.
2 Corinthians 4:16 CEV

TOP TEN FAILURES

Guess these top ten failures of all time (answers below):

10. The engineer who neglected to design a reverse gear in the first car he manufactured.

9. The group turned down by Decca Records because "guitars are on their way out."

8. The illustrator told by his newspaper editor to pursue another line of work.

7. The skinny kid who hated the way he looked and was always being beat up by bullies.

6. The seriously ill, deeply in debt composer who in desperation wrote an oratorio in a few hours.

5. The obese, bald, deformed eccentric who became a reclusive thinker.

4. The orchestra conductor-composer who made his greatest contributions after becoming deaf.

3. The politician who lost his first seven elections.

2. The boy everyone thought was mute because his stutter was so bad he never spoke until he was a teenager.

1. The woman born deaf and blind who became a great writer and philanthropist and once said, "I thank God for my handicaps."

Answers: 10. Henry Ford. 9. The Beatles. 8. Walt Disney. 7. Charles Atlas. 6. George Frederick Handel (*The Messiah*). 5. Socrates. 4. Ludwig von Beethoven. 3. Abraham Lincoln. 2. James Earl Jones. 1. Helen Keller.

Our greatest failures can produce our greatest successes.

FAITH

What is faith? It is the confident assurance that what we hope for is going to happen. It is the evidence of things we cannot yet see.

Hebrews 11:1 NLT

Above all, taking the shield of faith, wherewith ye shall be able to quench all the fiery darts of the wicked.

Ephesians 6:16 KJV

We walk by faith, not by sight.

2 Corinthians 5:7 NKJV

"Everything is possible for him who believes."

Mark 9:23

44

TREK ACROSS ANARCTICA

Early in the twentieth century, Sir Ernest Shackleford made a voyage to Antarctica. He had a dream of crossing the 2,100 miles of the icy continent by dogsled. Shackleford's ship, however, ran into an ice pack nearly 200 miles from land and sank.

He and his men trudged across drifting ice floes to reach land and then continued on to the nearest outpost, nearly 1,200 miles away. As they made their way on foot, they pulled behind them a ton of weight—a lifeboat containing the only supplies they were able to salvage from their sinking ship.

When they reached waters clear enough to navigate, they faced waves as high as ninety feet! They finally reached South Georgia Island and were told later that the expanse of water they crossed had never been crossed before.

Seven months after they set sail, the group finally reached their destination, the chosen point for beginning their trek across Antarctica. When asked about the experience, each man said that he had felt the presence of One unseen, who had guided them. Each man had a sense that he was not alone and that he would survive.

You're never alone; you'll make it! Take a bold step of faith, and watch what God will do.

FAITH

When I look at the night sky and see the work of your fingers—the moon and the stars you have set in place—what are mortals that you should think of us, mere humans that you should care for us? For you made us only a little lower than God, and you crowned us with glory and honor.

Psalm 8:3-5 NLT

46

Let love and faithfulness never leave you; bind them around your neck, write them on the tablet of your heart.

Proverbs 3:3

Every child of God can defeat the world, and our faith is what gives us this victory.

1 John 5:4 CEV

"His master said to him, 'Well done, good and faithful servant; you have been faithful over a little, I will set you over much; enter into the joy of your master.'"

Matthew 25:21 RSV

BEYOND HUMAN POSSIBILITY

Cathy Guisewite is the creator of the very popular syndicated cartoon strip "Cathy." In the comic strip, Cathy routinely has encounters with her mother, who is always full of advice for her unmarried, career-oriented daughter. In real-life, Cathy's mother has been known to offer her advice from time to time.

Guisewite once said:

I believe very strongly in visualizing goals way beyond what seems humanly possible. I got this from my parents. When my mother first suggested I submit some scribbles to a syndicate, I told her I knew nothing about comic strips. Mom said, "So what? You'll learn." When I pointed out that I didn't know how to draw, she said, "So what? You'll learn." All parents believe their children can do the impossible. They thought it the minute we were born, and no matter how hard we've tried to prove them wrong, they all think it about us now. And the really annoying thing is, they're probably right.

When we face challenges that lie just beyond our ability, we enter into the realm of faith and hope. It is as we face new frontiers in our lives that we truly encounter what our Creator has endowed us to do. Don't be afraid to desire to accomplish more in life.

FAMILY

Choose for yourselves this day whom you will
serve. . . . But as for me and my house, we will
serve the LORD.

Joshua 24:15 NKJV

Be ye kind one to another, tenderhearted,
forgiving one another, even as God for Christ's
sake hath forgiven you.

Ephesians 4:32 KJV

48

Teach a child to choose the right path, and when
he is older he will remain upon it.

Proverbs 22:6 TLB

Children, obey your parents in the Lord, for this is
right. "Honor your father and mother"—which is
the first commandment with a promise—"that it
may go well with you and that you may enjoy long
life on the earth."

Ephesians 6:1-3

NEVER

n *What Is a Family?* Edith Schaeffer writes:

We knew a family in Lausanne some twenty years ago, a mother with a son and daughter who sometimes lived with her at the then-temporary apartment and went to a day school—or sometimes went to boarding school. Father was an importer-exporter who traveled most of the time around and around the world. When the teenage girl asked, "Why, Dad, can't you ever be home? Why can't you do less and have some time together with us?" The reply was, "I have to earn enough . . . so that if I die you'll have enough." . . . That family lived in a "temporary" situation for years. . . . When did that man picture a family life being "normal"—when was the temporary portion going to end? We all know examples of homes where both father and mother work "until we get another car" or "until we pay for this house" or "until we buy a summer cottage" . . . months go by, years go by . . . never will these in my imaginary family know what it is like to have Mother open the front door or the kitchen door and say, "Hi! How was your day? Smell the bread baking? I'm making orange rolls. Come on in and have a glass of milk." Never.[2]

The best you can give your child is you.

FAMILY

He will direct his children and his household after him to keep the way of the LORD by doing what is right and just.

Genesis 18:19

Fathers, do not exasperate your children; instead, bring them up in the training and instruction of the Lord.

Ephesians 6:4

Be very careful never to forget what you have seen God doing for you. May his miracles have a deep and permanent effect upon your lives! Tell your children and your grandchildren about the glorious miracles he did.

Deuteronomy 4:9 TLB

If anyone does not provide for his own, and especially for those of his household, he has denied the faith and is worse than an unbeliever.

1 Timothy 5:8 NASB

50

WHOSE EXAMPLE?

According to legend, the apostle John had a tame partridge that he enjoyed feeding and tending. A serious hunter passed by one day and was astonished to see the great apostle playing with a pet bird. He said, "I am surprised, sir, to see you engaged in such an amusement when there are such great matters related to the Gospel with which you could be busy."

The apostle asked in return, "Do you always keep your bow bent?"

The hunter replied, "Why, no. That would render it useless. I loosen the string unless I am hunting."

The apostle nodded and said, "So I unbend my mind for the same reason."

One summer, a pastor announced that he wasn't going to take a vacation since the devil never goes on vacation. A parishioner went home and reread the Gospels to see if Jesus had the same attitude. He found that in His three years of active ministry, Jesus had ten periods of retirement away from the crowds in addition to nightly rest and Sabbath-day rest! He asked his pastor the next Sunday, "Are you following the devil's example or the Lord's?"

Take time to rest and play with your family. Recreation is just that, recreation—a time to renew your energy, as well as your most valuable relationships.

FAVOR

Never tire of loyalty and kindness. Hold these virtues tightly. Write them deep within your heart. If you want favor with both God and man, and a reputation for good judgment and common sense, then trust the Lord completely; don't ever trust yourself. In everything you do, put God first, and he will direct you and crown your efforts with success.

Proverbs 3:3-6 TLB

Surely, O LORD, you bless the righteous; you surround them with your favor as with a shield.

Psalm 5:12

A good name is to be chosen rather than great riches, Loving favor rather than silver and gold.

Proverbs 22:1 NKJV

Whoever finds me [wisdom] finds life and wins approval from the Lord.

Proverbs 8:35 TLB

KINDNESS RETURNS

Many years ago, an elderly man and his wife entered the lobby of a small Philadelphia hotel. "Every guest room is taken," the clerk said but then added, "I can't send a nice couple like you out into the rain, though. Would you be willing to sleep in my room?"

The next morning, the elderly man said to the clerk, "You are the kind of man who should be the boss of the best hotel in the United States. Maybe someday I'll build one for you." The clerk laughed and forgot about the incident. Two years later, however, he received a letter containing a round-trip ticket to New York and a request that he be the guest of the elderly couple.

Once in New York, the old man led the clerk to the corner of Fifth Avenue and Thirty-fourth Street, where he pointed to an incredible new building and declared, "That is the hotel I have just built for you to manage." The young man, George C. Boldt, accepted the offer of William Waldorf Astor to become the manager of the original Waldorf-Astoria Hotel.

Good leaders will go out of their way to help people, and as a result, they will not only receive their favor but also the favor of others and—most importantly—the favor of God.

FAVOR

They did not conquer by their own strength and skill, but by your mighty power and because you smiled upon them and favored them.

Psalm 44:3 TLB

Jesus grew in wisdom and stature, and in favor with God and men.

Luke 2:52

In his distress he sought the favor of the LORD his God and humbled himself greatly before the God of his fathers.

2 Chronicles 33:12

God was with him and delivered him out of all his troubles, and gave him favor and wisdom in the presence of Pharaoh, king of Egypt; and he made him governor over Egypt and all his house.

Acts 7:9-10 NKJV

QUALIFIED BY WILLINGNESS

Although he was raised in church, Dwight was almost totally ignorant of the Bible when he moved to Boston to make his fortune. There, he began attending a Bible-preaching church. In April of 1855, a Sunday school teacher came to the store where Dwight worked. He simply and persuasively urged him to trust in the Lord Jesus.

Dwight did as the man instructed, and a month later he applied to become a church member. One fact was obvious to all: Dwight knew little of the Scriptures. His Sunday school teacher later wrote, "I think the committee of the church seldom met an applicant for membership who seemed more unlikely ever to become a Christian of clear and decided views of gospel truth, still less to fill any space of public or extended usefulness."

However, Dwight had favor with the committee. He was asked to undertake a year of study, which he did. Yet at his second interview, his answers to the deacons were only slightly improved. He still was only barely literate, and his spoken grammar was atrocious.

Few would have thought God could ever use a person like Dwight. But God saw in the willingness of Dwight L. Moody all the raw material necessary to create a major spokesman for His Word. He found favor with God.

Strive to have this same attitude of willingness, so that you, too, will have favor with God. Then, watch as He molds you into a strong and effective leader.

FEAR

My flesh and my heart may fail, But God is the
strength of my heart and my portion forever.

Psalm 73:26 NASB

In the day of my trouble I will call upon You,
For You will answer me.

Psalm 86:7 NKJV

Let us be bold, then, and say, "The Lord is my
helper, I will not be afraid. What can anyone
do to me?"

Hebrews 13:6 TEV

God hath not given us the spirit of fear; but of
power, and of love, and of a sound mind.

2 Timothy 1:7 KJV

TAKING A RISK

One simply cannot live without taking risks. Risk is woven into every aspect of our daily experience!

- To laugh is to risk appearing the fool.
- To weep is to risk appearing sentimental.
- To reach out for another is to risk involvement.
- To expose feelings is to risk exposing our true selves.
- To place your ideas, your dreams, before the crowd is to risk loss.
- To love is to risk not being loved in return.
- To live is to risk dying.
- To hope is to risk despair.
- To try at all is to risk failure.

—Unknown

Even so, the greatest hazard in life is to risk nothing. Because the person who risks nothing:

- accomplishes nothing,
- has nothing,
- feels nothing,
- and in the end, becomes nothing.

Don't be afraid to take a calculated risk. Risk is essential for growth in every area of life.

FEAR

GOD is our refuge and strength,
A very present help in trouble.
Therefore we will not fear, though the
earth should change
And though the mountains slip into the
heart of the sea.

Psalm 46:1-2 NASB

58

My slanderers pursue me all day long; many are
attacking me in their pride. When I am afraid, I will
trust in you. In God, whose word I praise, in God
I trust; I will not be afraid. What can mortal man
do to me?

Psalm 56:2-4

That he would grant unto us, that we being
delivered out of the hand of our enemies might
serve him without fear.

Luke 1:74 KJV

Be glad for the chance to suffer as Christ suffered.
It will prepare you for even greater happiness when
he makes his glorious return. Count it a blessing
when you suffer for being a Christian. This shows
that God's glorious Spirit is with you.

1 Peter 4:13-14 CEV

JUST SAY NO

A teenager named Buck was walking to his father's apartment from a subway stop one day when he suddenly realized that two men were flanking him.

"Give me your wallet," one of the men insisted. "I have a gun. Give me your wallet, or I'll shoot."

"No," Buck said.

"Hey, man, you don't understand. We're robbing you. Give me your wallet."

"No."

"Give me your wallet, or I'll knife you."

"No."

"Give me your wallet, or we'll beat you up." By now the robber was pleading more than he was demanding.

"No," Buck said once again. He kept walking, and a few steps later he realized that the two men had disappeared.

As he related this story to a friend, the friend asked, "Weren't you scared?"

Buck replied, "Of course I was scared!"

"Then why didn't you give them your wallet?"

"Because," Buck answered matter-of-factly, "my learner's permit is in it."

While it may be wise to give in to the demands of a thief, the first and best answer to fear is always no!

FORGIVENESS

Let the wicked leave their way of life and change
their way of thinking. Let them turn to the LORD,
our God; he is merciful and quick to forgive.

Isaiah 55:7 TEV

"Come now, and let us reason together,"
Says the LORD,
"Though your sins are as scarlet,
They will be as white as snow;
Though they are red like crimson,
They will be like wool."

Isaiah 1:18 NASB

Blessed is he whose transgressions are forgiven,
whose sins are covered.

Psalm 32:1

Be kind to each other, tenderhearted, forgiving one
another, just as God has forgiven you because you
belong to Christ.

Ephesians 4:32 TLB

WORKING THROUGH THE HURT

loyd John Ogilvie wrote the following in *Let God Love You:*

> The hardest time to be gentle is when we know we are right and someone else is obviously dead wrong. . . . But the greatest temptation for most of us is when someone has failed us and has admitted it, and their destiny or happiness is in our hands. We hold the power to give or refuse a blessing. Recently, a dear friend hurt me in both word and action. Each time we met I almost began to enjoy the leverage of being the offended one. His first overtures of restitution were resisted because of the gravity of the judgment I had made. The most difficult thing was to surrender my indignation and work through my hurt. Finally, the Lord got me where He wanted me. . . . "Lloyd, why is it so important to you who gets the credit, just so My work gets done?" I gave up my right to be what only God could be as this man's judge and savior. The gentle attitude began to flow.[3]

When we withhold forgiveness, we not only hurt the person we don't want to forgive, we also hurt ourselves. We lose the joy of living. When we forgive, we release peace and restoration to the forgiven and to ourselves.

FORGIVENESS

If we confess our sins, he is faithful and just to forgive us our sins, and to cleanse us from all unrighteousness.

1 John 1:9 KJV

You, LORD, are good, and ready to forgive, And abundant in mercy to all those who call upon You.

Psalm 86:5 NKJV

[The LORD declares]: "I am the One who forgives all your sins, for my sake; I will not remember your sins."

Isaiah 43:25 NCV

If my people will humble themselves and pray, and search for me, and turn from their wicked ways, I will hear them from heaven and forgive their sins and heal their land.

2 Chronicles 7:14 TLB

MOST GENEROUS TREATMENT

In his book, *Beneath the Cross of Jesus,* A. Leonard Griffith tells the story of a young Korean exchange student, a leader in Christian circles at the University of Pennsylvania, who left his apartment on the evening of April 25, 1958, to mail a letter to his parents. As he turned from the mailbox, he was met by eleven leather-jacketed teenage boys. Without a word, they beat him with a blackjack, a lead pipe, and their shoes and fists—and left him lying dead in the gutter.

All of Philadelphia cried out for vengeance. The district attorney planned to seek the death penalty for the arrested youth. And then, this letter arrived, signed by the boy's parents and twenty other relatives in Korea:

Our family has met together and we have decided to petition that the most generous treatment possible within the laws of your government be given to those who have committed this criminal action. . . . In order to give evidence of our sincere hope contained in this petition, we have decided to save money to start a fund to be used for the religious, educational, vocational, and social guidance of the boys when they are released. . . . We have dared to express our hope with a spirit received from the gospel of our Savior Jesus Christ who died for our sins.

When you forgive, you are no longer the victim but rather the victor.

FRIENDSHIP

A friend loveth at all times.

Proverbs 17:17 KJV

[Jesus said]: "No longer do I call you servants, for a servant does not know what his master is doing; but I have called you friends, for all things that I heard from My Father I have made known to you."

John 15:15 NKJV

64

Two are better than one, because they have a good return for their work: If one falls down, his friend can help him up.

Ecclesiastes 4:9-10

A man of many friends comes to ruin, But there is a friend who sticks closer than a brother.

Proverbs 18:24 NASB

REACH OUT IN FRIENDSHIP

More than 95 percent of all Americans receive at least one Christmas card each year. The average is actually more than seventy cards per family! Millions of cards are mailed each holiday season throughout the world. Have you ever wondered where this custom originated?

A museum director in the mid-nineteenth century liked to send yearly notes to his friends at Christmastime, just to wish them a joyful holiday season. One year, he found he had little time to write, yet he still wanted to send a message of good cheer. He asked his friend John Horsely to design a card that he might sign and send. Those who received the cards loved the idea and created cards of their own. And thus, the Christmas card was invented!

It's often the simple, heartfelt gestures in life that speak most loudly of friendship. Ask yourself today, *What can I do to bring a smile to the face of a friend? What can I do to bring good cheer into the life of a friend who is needy, troubled, sick, or sorrowing?* Follow through on your inspiration, and remember, it's not a gift you are giving as much as a friendship you are building!

FRIENDSHIP

"Abraham believed God, and it was credited to him as righteousness," and he was called God's friend.

James 2:23

Wounds from a friend are better than kisses from an enemy!

Proverbs 27:6 TLB

"The greatest love you can have for your friends is to give your life for them. And you are my friends if you do what I command you."

John 15:13-14 TEV

The sweet smell of perfume and oils is pleasant, and so is good advice from a friend.

Proverbs 27:9 NCV

FRIENDS MAKE FRIENDS

The complex shapes of snowflakes have confounded scientists for centuries. In the past, scientists believed that the making of a snowflake was a two-step process. They believed that inside the winds of a winter storm, a microscopic speck of dust would become trapped in a molecule of water vapor. Scientists suggested that this particle would then become heavily frosted with droplets of super-cooled water and plunge to earth. During its descent, the varying temperature and humidity would sculpt the heavy, icy crystal into a lacy snowflake. Or at least that's what scientists used to believe.

In recent decades, the true formation of the snowflake was discovered. Very few snowflakes actually contain dust or other particles. Dr. John Hallett, of the University of Nevada, discovered that the majority of snowflakes are formed from fragments of other snowflakes. As snowflakes are formed, extremely dry or cold air causes them to break up into smaller parts. The small fragments then act as seeds for new snowflakes to develop. Most of snow is made, therefore, by snow!

In like manner, friendly people generate friends. Their neighborly outlook inspires others to reach out and be friendly too. Pass along the seed of friendship, and watch what develops in your own life.

FRUSTRATION

Call to Me, and I will answer you, and show you great and mighty things, which you do not know.

Jeremiah 33:3 NKJV

We know that all things work together for good to them that love God, to them who are the called according to his purpose.

Romans 8:28 KJV

Encourage the exhausted, and strengthen the feeble. Say to those with anxious heart, "Take courage, fear not. Behold, your God will come."

Isaiah 35:3-4 NASB

God is faithful; he will not let you be tempted beyond what you can bear. But when you are tempted, he will also provide a way out so that you can stand up under it.

1 Corinthians 10:13

NOT HOME YET

On their way home from a lifetime of service as missionaries in Africa, an elderly couple found themselves on the same ocean liner as President Teddy Roosevelt, who was returning from a big-game hunting expedition.

The couple watched in awe at the fanfare given the president and his entourage. When the ship docked in New York, a band was waiting to greet him, the mayor was there to welcome him, and the newspapers heralded his return.

Meanwhile, the missionary couple slipped quietly off the ship and found a cheap apartment. They had no pension, they were in poor health, and they were discouraged and fearful. The husband, especially, could not seem to get over how President Roosevelt had received such acclaim, while their decades of service had gone without notice or reward. "God isn't treating us fairly," he complained bitterly to his wife.

"Why don't you pray about it?" his wife advised.

A short time later, the wife noticed a change in her husband's demeanor. "What happened?" she asked.

The man replied, "The Lord put His hand on my shoulder and simply said, 'But you're not home yet!'"

FRUSTRATION

The LORD says, "My thoughts are not like your thoughts. Your ways are not like my ways."
Isaiah 55:8 NCV

If God is on our side, who can ever be against us? Since he did not spare even his own Son for us but gave him up for us all, won't he also surely give us everything else?
Romans 8:31-32 TLB

70

I will make an eternal covenant with them. I will never stop doing good things for them, and I will make them fear me with all their heart, so that they will never turn away from me.
Jeremiah 32:40 TEV

Though I walk in the midst of trouble,
You will revive me;
You will stretch out Your hand
Against the wrath of my enemies,
And Your right hand will save me.
The LORD will perfect that which concerns me.
Psalm 138:7-8 NKJV

DOING WHAT HE COULD DO

Sparky didn't have much going for him. He failed every subject in the eighth grade, and in high school, he flunked Latin, algebra, English, and physics. He made the golf team but promptly lost the only important match of the season, and then he lost the consolation match. He was awkward socially—more shy than disliked. He never once asked a girl to go out on a date in high school.

One thing, however, was important to Sparky— drawing. He was proud of his artwork even though no one else appreciated it. He submitted cartoons to the editors of his high school yearbook, but they were rejected. Even so, Sparky aspired to be an artist. After high school, he sent samples of his artwork to the Walt Disney Studios. Again, his work was rejected.

Still, Sparky didn't quit! He decided to write his own autobiography in cartoons. The popularity of his cartoon strip eventually led to countless books, television shows, and licensing opportunities. Sparky, you see, was Charles Schulz, creator of the "Peanuts" comic strip. Like his main character, Charlie Brown, Schulz seemed unable to succeed at many things. But he made the most of his talent and refused to quit.

So the next time you are faced with criticism, choose to believe in yourself, and never give up on your dreams!

GIVING

He who gives to the poor will lack nothing, but he who closes his eyes to them receives many curses.
Proverbs 28:27

"Give to everyone who asks you, and if anyone takes what belongs to you, do not demand it back."
Luke 6:30

72

"Give, and it will be given to you. A good measure, pressed down, shaken together and running over, will be poured into your lap. For with the measure you use, it will be measured to you."
Luke 6:38

Each man should give what he has decided in his heart to give, not reluctantly or under compulsion, for God loves a cheerful giver.
2 Corinthians 9:7

HONEYCOMB GIVERS

There are three kinds of givers: the flint, the sponge, and the honeycomb. Which kind are you?

To get anything from the flint, you must hammer it. Yet, all you generally get are chips and sparks. The flint gives nothing away if it can help it and even then only with a great display.

To get anything from the sponge, you must squeeze it. It readily yields to pressure, and the more it is pressed, the more it gives. Still, you must push.

To get anything from the honeycomb, however, you must only take what freely flows from it. It gives its sweetness generously, dripping on all without pressure, without begging or badgering.

Note, too, that there is another difference in the honeycomb. It is a renewable resource. Unlike the flint or sponge, the honeycomb is connected to life; it is the product of the ongoing work and creative energy of bees.

If you are a "honeycomb giver," your life will be continually replenished as you give. And as long as you are connected to the Source of all life, you can never run dry. When you give freely, you will receive in like manner so that whatever you give away will soon be multiplied back to you.

GIVING

Remember this: Whoever sows sparingly will also reap sparingly, and whoever sows generously will also reap generously. Each man should give what he has decided in his heart to give, not reluctantly or under compulsion, for God loves a cheerful giver. And God is able to make all grace abound to you, so that in all things at all times, having all that you need, you will abound in every good work.

2 Corinthians 9:6-8

In all things I have shown you that by so toiling one must help the weak, remembering the words of the Lord Jesus, how he said, "It is more blessed to give than to receive."

Acts 20:35 RSV

Yes, ascribe to the Lord
The glory due his name!
Bring an offering and come before him;
Worship the Lord when clothed with holiness!

1 Chronicles 16:29 TLB

"Whoever can be trusted with very little can also be trusted with much, and whoever is dishonest with very little will also be dishonest with much. So if you have not been trustworthy in handling worldly wealth, who will trust you with true riches?"

Luke 16:10-11

74

GRATEFUL GIVING

The story is told of a man and woman who gave a sizable contribution to their church to honor the memory of their son who lost his life in the war. When the generous donation was announced to the congregation, a woman whispered to her husband, "Let's give the same amount in honor of each of our boys."

The husband replied, "What are you talking about? Neither one of our sons was killed in the war."

"Exactly," said the woman. "Let's give it as an expression of our gratitude to God for sparing their lives!"

All of our charitable giving in life produces the following benefits:

- It helps those in need.
- It inspires others to give.
- And it builds character in us—selflessness, temperance, generosity, and compassion.

Keep in mind that when you give, you are ultimately giving to people, even though your gift might be made to an institution or organization. Your giving not only brings sunshine to the lives of others but to your own life as well.

GUIDANCE

Ask the LORD to bless your plans, and you will be successful in carrying them out.

Proverbs 16:3 TEV

The steps of a good man are ordered by the LORD: and he delighteth in his way.

Psalm 37:23 KJV

I am always with you; you hold me by my right hand. You guide me with your counsel, and afterward you will take me into glory.

Psalm 73:23-24

I will instruct you (says the Lord) and guide you along the best pathway for your life; I will advise you and watch your progress.

Psalm 32:8 TLB

CUTTING OUT CRITICISM

n *A Closer Walk*, Catherine Marshall writes:

One morning last week He [God] gave me an assignment: for one day I was to go on a "fast" from criticism. I was not to criticize anybody about anything. For the first half of the day, I simply felt a void, almost as if I had been wiped out as a person. This was especially true at lunch. . . . I listened to the others and kept silent. . . . In our talkative family no one seemed to notice. Bemused, I noticed that my comments were not missed. The federal government, the judicial system, and the institutional church could apparently get along fine without my penetrating observations. But still I didn't see what this fast on criticism was accomplishing—until mid-afternoon. That afternoon, a specific, positive vision for this life was dropped into my mind with God's unmistakable hallmark on it—joy! Ideas began to flow in a way I had not experienced in years. Now it was apparent what the Lord wanted me to see. My critical nature had not corrected a single one of the multitudinous things I found fault with. What it had done was stifle my own creativity.[4]

Ask God for guidance each day. Ask Him to reveal weaknesses in your character so that with His help, you will be able to reach your full potential.

GUIDANCE

This God is our God for ever and ever; he will be our guide even to the end.

Psalm 48:14

The LORD will continually guide you,
And satisfy your desire in scorched places,
And give strength to your bones;
And you will be like a watered garden,
And like a spring of water whose waters do not fail.

Isaiah 58:11 NASB

78

Trust in the LORD with all thine heart; and lean not unto thine own understanding. In all thy ways acknowledge him, and he shall direct thy paths.

Proverbs 3:5-6 KJV

Show me your ways, O LORD, teach me your paths; guide me in your truth and teach me.

Psalm 25:4-5

RULES FOR VICTORIOUS LIVING

There are plenty of things in this world that can keep you from living victoriously. Follow these rules, and you will find that the right attitude can help you overcome these obstacles.

- When people are unreasonable, illogical, self-centered, and arrogant, love them anyway.
- When people insist that your goodness contains selfish ulterior motives, do good deeds anyway.
- When you are successful, people may become jealous of you. Succeed anyway.
- When you are honest and frank, some may seek to twist your words against you. Be honest and frank anyway.
- When you do good deeds today, some may forget about it by tomorrow. Do good deeds anyway.
- When you show yourself to be a big person with great ideas, don't be surprised if you are opposed by small people with closed minds. Think big anyway.
- When someone seeks to destroy overnight what you have spent years building, build anyway.

Mark Twain once said, "Always do right. This will gratify most people, and astonish the rest!"

HONESTY

Ye shall not steal, neither deal falsely, neither lie one to another.

Leviticus 19:11 KJV

That no man go beyond and defraud his brother in any matter: because that the Lord is the avenger of all such, as we also have forewarned you and testified. For God hath not called us unto uncleanness, but unto holiness.

1 Thesalonians 4:6-7 KJV

Better is a little with righteousness than great revenues without right.

Proverbs 16:8 KJV

He that walketh righteously, and speaketh uprightly; he that despiseth the gain of oppressions, that shaketh his hands from holding of bribes, that stoppeth his ears from hearing of blood, and shutteth his eyes from seeing evil; he shall dwell on high; his place of defense shall be the munitions of rocks: bread shall be given him; his waters shall be sure.

Isaiah 33:15-16 KJV

THE GREATEST ASSET

The former president of Baylor University, Rufus C. Burleson, once told an audience:

How often I have heard my father paint in glowing words the honesty of his old friend Colonel Ben Sherrod. When he was threatened with bankruptcy and destitution in old age and was staggering under a debt of $850,000, a contemptible lawyer told him, "Colonel Sherrod, you are hopelessly ruined, but if you will furnish me $5,000 as a witness fee, I can pick a technical flaw in the whole thing and get you out of it." The grand old Alabamian said, "Your proposition is insulting. I signed the notes in good faith, and the last dollar shall be paid if charity digs my grave and buys my shroud." He carried me and my brother Richard once especially to see that incorruptible old man, and his face and words are imprinted upon my heart and brain.

People remember when you keep your promises, and they also remember when you don't. They remember when you tell the truth, especially when you could have profited by being less honest. Honesty is your greatest asset and your best virtue. It is the measure by which most people will make their judgments about your character.

HONESTY

Lie not one to another, seeing that ye have put off the old man with his deeds; and have put on the new man, which is renewed in knowledge after the image of him that created him.

Colossians 3:9-10 KJV

The wicked borroweth, and payeth not again: but the righteous sheweth mercy, and giveth.

Psalm 37:21 KJV

Withhold not good from them to whom it is due, when it is in the power of thine hand to do *it*.

Proverbs 3:27 KJV

The integrity of the upright guides them, but the crookedness of the treacherous destroys them.

Proverbs 11:3 RSV

A TEMPTING OFFER

George Jones began his career as a clerk in a crockery store. He soon gained a reputation as being a bright, ambitious employee—a young man known for good work habits, fine manners, and an easy-going personality. The foremost traits people referred to when praising George, however, were his honesty and trustworthiness. It was this reputation that came to the attention of Henry J. Raymond, a renowned journalist, and together Raymond and Jones started the *New York Times*.

Mr. Jones continued to live up to his reputation. His loyalty to Raymond and his honesty as a businessman won him great repute in New York City.

Then the *Times* began a crusade against Boss Tweed and his corrupt dynasty. Jones received an under-the-table offer of $500,000—a vast sum at the time—from associates of Tweed. All he had to do was retire to Europe. "You can live like a prince the rest of your days," the man making the offer said. But Jones replied, "Yes, and know myself every day to be a rascal."

A clean conscience can't be bought. That is what makes it so highly valued! Keeping a clean conscience is as simple as deciding to do so. Decide not to let tempting offers influence you. Remember that God is always there to give you the strength to overcome any temptation.

HOPE

Behold, the eye of the LORD is upon them that fear him, upon them that hope in his mercy.

Psalm 33:18 KJV

It is good that one should hope and wait quietly For the salvation of the LORD.

Lamentations 3:26 NKJV

Happy is he whole help is the God of Jacob, whose hope is in the LORD his God.

Psalm 146:5 RSV

Christ has also introduced us to God's undeserved kindness on which we take our stand. So we are happy, as we look forward to sharing in the glory of God.

Romans 5:2 CEV

STARTING OVER

He had been expelled from college, and his business attempts had failed. Now, as he stood on the windswept shores of Lake Michigan one wintry night, the thirty-two-year-old man took one last look up at the sky as he prepared to jump into the icy water.

It was an overpowering moment. He felt a rush of awe as he saw the starry heavens, and the thought seared his mind, *You have no right to eliminate yourself. You do not belong to you.* R. Buckminster Fuller walked away from the lake and started over.

From that point on, he embarked on a journey that led him into careers as an inventor, engineer, mathematician, architect, poet, and cosmologist. He eventually won dozens of honorary degrees and a Nobel Prize nomination. Fuller invented the geodesic dome, wrote two dozen books, circled the globe fifty-seven times, and told millions about his dreams for the future. He seldom repeated himself in lectures that sometimes lasted three to four hours on topics that ranged from education to the origin of life.

The day Buckminster Fuller encountered hope was the day he began to find meaning for his life. There is always a reason to hope. Hope gives us the strength to walk away from failure and move on to success.

HOPE

Praise be to the God and Father of our Lord Jesus Christ! In his great mercy he has given us new birth into a living hope through the resurrection of Jesus Christ from the dead, and into an inheritance that can never perish, spoil or fade—kept in heaven for you.

1 Peter 1:3-4

O Lord, you alone are my hope. I've trusted you, O LORD, from childhood.

Psalm 71:5 NLT

When they see me waiting, expecting your Word, those who fear you will take heart and be glad.

Psalm 119:74
THE MESSAGE

Hope in God and wait expectantly for Him, for I shall yet praise Him, my Help and my God.

Psalm 42:5 AMP

SELLING INEXPERIENCE

A young man once placed this ad in a New York City newspaper:

Inexperience is the most valuable thing a man can bring to a new job. A man of inexperience, you see, is forced to rely upon imagination and verve, instead of timeworn routine and formula. If you're in the kind of business that is penalized by routine and formula thinking, then I'd like to work for you. Inexperience is my forte. I'm twenty-five-years-old and have the ability to become enthusiastic and emotionally involved in my work.

That young man was immediately hired by a chain of photo studios. He had successfully transformed a negative into a positive by finding a way to make his inexperience work for him. He viewed life with enthusiasm and hope rather than discouragement and defeat, and others were drawn to him.

Be enthusiastic and hopeful about every area of your life—your family, your friends, your coworkers, your work, your hobbies, your church, but especially your dreams and your potential to achieve them. Enthusiasm and hope will kindle new joy in your life and cause others to be drawn to you. Soon you will find yourself receiving unique opportunities, sound advice, and valuable resources.

HOSPITALITY

In all things I have shown you that by so toiling one must help the weak, remembering the words of the Lord Jesus, how he said, "It is more blessed to give than to receive."

Acts 20:35 RSV

When God's children are in need, be the one to help them out. And get into the habit of inviting guests home for dinner or, if they need lodging, for the night.

Romans 12:13 NLT

Be hospitable to one another without grumbling.

1 Peter 4:9 NKJV

Dear children, let us not love with words or tongue but with actions and in truth.

1 John 3:18

A MIGHTY TREE

Christian man was walking to church one night when he encountered four boys loitering on the street corner. He invited them to go to the service with him. They did, and each of the boys also agreed to return to church with him the next Sunday. They became the nucleus of a Sunday school class the man began to teach.

Years later, a group of the man's friends decided to try to contact the four boys to see what had happened in their lives and to invite them to write a special birthday letter to their teacher to be read at a surprise party. Their letters revealed that one of them had become a missionary to China, one was the president of the Federal Reserve Bank, one was the private secretary to President Herbert Hoover, and the fourth was President Hoover himself!

If you were to hold a handful of pine nuts in your hand today, you could not begin to predict which of the seeds might actually sprout and produce a giant tree. It is amazing that such a large tree might grow from such a small seed. The only way to tell which nuts have trees inside them is to plant them! When you plant acts of kindness and generosity to others, you never know what mighty tree may grow from that small seed.

HOSPITALITY

Cheerfully share your home with those who need a meal or a place to stay.

1 Peter 4:9 NLT

"I tell you the truth, anyone who gives you a cup of water in my name because you belong to Christ will certainly not lose his reward."

Mark 9:41

Be sure to welcome strangers into your home. By doing this, some people have welcomed angels as guests, without even knowing it.

Hebrews 13:2 CEV

It's good work you're doing, helping these travelers on their way, hospitality worthy of God himself!

3 John 1:8 THE MESSAGE

BOTTOM DOLLAR

In *McKinney Living*, Robert J. Duncan tells the story of a friend named Cam who attended the final performance of the Grand Ole Opry at the Ryman Auditorium. When he found himself backstage with an acquaintance, he quickly asked the various stars there to sign the only piece of paper he could find—a one-dollar bill. That dollar bill became Cam's prized possession.

One morning in the bitter winter of 1976-77, Cam left the station where he worked and noticed a young man sitting in an old yellow Dodge. The car was still there the next day, and the next. Cam asked if something was wrong, and the man told him he had arrived in town for a job that didn't begin for three more days. He had no food and no place to stay. Reluctantly, he asked Cam if he might borrow a dollar. Cam told him he was down to his last dime, but then recalled his Grand Ole Opry dollar. He gave it spontaneously.

The next day, Cam got a job paying $500 for two hours' work. More opportunities began to flow his way. Eventually, Cam was back on his feet financially. He never again saw the man in the old yellow car. Cam only knew that whoever the man was and whatever principle was in effect, things happened when he gave his "bottom dollar."[5]

IMPURE THOUGHTS

Set your mind on things above, not on things on the earth.

Colossians 3:2 NKJV

Jesus turned on Peter and said, " . . . You are a dangerous trap to me. You are thinking merely from a human point of view, and not from God's."

Matthew 16:23 TLB

92

We pull down every proud obstacle that is raised against the knowledge of God; we take every thought captive and make it obey Christ.

2 Corinthians 10:5 TEV

The thoughts of the wicked are an abomination to the LORD: but the words of the pure are pleasant words.

Proverbs 15:26 KJV

THINKING AND DOING

During a national spelling bee in Washington, D.C., eleven-year-old Rosalie Elliot, a champion from South Carolina, was asked to spell the word *avowal*. Her soft southern accent made it difficult for the judges to determine if she had used an *a* or an *e* in the last syllable of the word. The judges deliberated for several minutes and listened to taped playbacks, but still they couldn't determine which letter had been used. Finally the chief judge asked Rosalie, "Was the letter an *a* or an *e*?"

Rosalie knew by now the correct spelling of the word and realized that she had misspelled it. If she lied, she could continue; if she told the truth, she would lose. While some may have chosen to win at any cost, Rosalie's conscience told her how to reply. Without hesitation, Rosalie replied that she had misspelled the word and had used an *e*. As she walked from the stage, the entire audience stood and applauded her honesty.

We often think that who we *are* determines our actions. More often than not, however, what we *think* determines what we do. And what you think today will determine what you will do and who you will become tomorrow.

IMPURE THOUGHTS

To be carnally minded is death; but to be spiritually minded is life and peace.

Romans 8:6 KJV

Let the wicked forsake his way
And the unrighteous man his thoughts;
And let him return to the LORD.

Isaiah 55:7 NASB

94

The word of God is alive and active, sharper than any double-edged sword. It cuts all the way through, to where soul and spirit meet, to where joints and marrow come together. It judges the desires and thoughts of the heart.

Hebrews 4:12 TEV

Let the peace that Christ gives control your thinking, because you were all called together in one body to have peace.

Colossians 3:15 NCV

A MOTHBALLED CONSCIENCE

Norman Vincent Peale once stayed home for a month while his wife and children went on vacation. About midway through that month, Peale met a beautiful girl looking for excitement. When she made it clear that she would like to go on a date with Peale, he "put his conscience in mothballs" and arranged to meet her on Saturday night.

Peale awoke on Saturday morning and decided to take a walk on the beach. He took an old ax along to chop some rope away from the wreck of an old barge that had washed up on the shore. Due to the freshness of the morning and the rhythm of the ax, Peale began to chop in earnest.

As he chopped, a strange thing began to happen. He said, "I felt as if I were outside myself, looking at myself through a kind of fog that was gradually clearing. Suddenly I knew that what I had been planning for that evening was so wrong, so out of keeping with the innermost me." Peale promptly cancelled the date.

Take a good look at the choices you make. Promptly reconsider any that contradict your conscience, and ask God for a clearer view on the right way to proceed.

JEALOUSY

When you follow your own wrong inclinations
your lives will produce these evil results:
. . . hatred and fighting, jealousy and anger,
constant effort to get the best for yourself.

Galatians 5:19-20 TLB

A relaxed attitude lengthens life; jealousy rots
it away.

Proverbs 14:30 NLT

96

Let us behave decently, as in the daytime, not in
orgies and drunkenness, not in sexual immorality
and debauchery, not in dissension and jealousy.

Romans 13:13

Anger is cruel and destroys like a flood, but no
one can put up with jealousy!

Proverbs 27:4 NCV

BE A BEE

Some people let jealousy rule their emotions. They seem to go through their days with their "stingers out," ready to attack others or to defend their positions at the slightest provocation. We should remember, however, the full nature of the "bees" we sometimes seem to emulate.

Bees readily feed each other. The worker bees feed the queen bee, who cannot feed herself. They feed the drones while they work in the hive. They feed their young. Bees will even feed bees from different colonies.

In cold weather, bees cluster together for warmth. They fan their wings to cool the hive in hot weather, thus working for one another's comfort.

When the bees must move to new quarters, scouts report back to the group, performing a dance like the one used to report a find of flowers. When enough scouts have confirmed the suitability of the new location, the bees appear to make a common decision, take wing, and migrate together in what we call a swarm. Their communal caring for each other leaves no room for jealousy.

Bees engage their stingers only as a last-resort measure of self-defense, but they never use them against their fellow bees. We would do well to learn from them!

JEALOUSY

Jealousy enrages a man, And he will not spare
in the day of vengeance.

Proverbs 6:34 NASB

When the Jewish leaders saw the crowds, they were
jealous, and cursed and argued against whatever
Paul said.

Acts 13:45 TLB

98

Jacob's sons became jealous of Joseph and sold
him to be a slave in Egypt.

Acts 7:9 NCV

When there is jealousy among you and you quarrel
with one another, doesn't this prove that you
belong to this world, living by its standards?

1 Corinthians 3:3 TEV

MINING FOR GOLD

Andrew Carnegie, considered to be one of the first to emphasize self-esteem and the potential for inner greatness, was famous for his ability to produce millionaires from among his employees. One day a reporter asked him, "How do you account for the fact you have forty-three millionaires working for you?"

Carnegie replied, "They weren't rich when they came. We work with people the same way you mine gold. You have to remove a lot of dirt before you find a small amount of gold."

Andrew Carnegie knew how to bring about change in people. He inspired them to develop their hidden treasure within and then watched with encouragement as their lives became transformed. He responded to their growth with enthusiasm instead of envy.

Many times we respond to others' successes with a negative complaint of "Why them? Why not me?" Envious of someone else's position, status, or abilities, we may even resort to bitter comments about them. Our energies would be better spent reviewing our own lives and looking for the gold hidden inside ourselves.

Effective leaders follow Andrew Carnegie's example of encouraging others in their successes. They adopt an attitude of enthusiasm instead of jealousy, and as a result, everyone benefits.

JOY

Ye shall go out with joy, and be led forth with peace: the mountains and the hills shall break forth before you into singing, and all the trees of the field shall clap their hands.

Isaiah 55:12 KJV

Blessed is the people that know the joyful sound: they shall walk, O LORD, in the light of thy countenance. In thy name shall they rejoice all the day: and in thy righteousness shall they be exalted.

Psalm 89:15-16 KJV

The voice of rejoicing and salvation is in the tabernacles of the righteous: the right hand of the LORD doeth valiantly.

Psalm 118:15 KJV

"These things have I spoken unto you, that my joy might remain in you, and that your joy might be full."

John 15:11 KJV

A MATCH MADE IN HEAVEN

Two women who lived in a convalescent center had each suffered an incapacitating stroke. Maggie's stroke had caused paralysis on her left side. Rachel's stroke had caused permanent damage to her right side. Both women were devastated by what had happened to them since they assumed they would never be able to pursue a pastime they had genuinely enjoyed throughout life—playing the piano.

Then one day, Maggie and Rachel met and began talking about their lives. When they realized they both had an interest in music, an idea emerged. When approached with the idea, the convalescent center's director brought them a piano and helped each woman sit on an elongated bench in front of it. Maggie played the right-hand notes while Rachel played the left-hand! Not only did they make beautiful music together, but they formed a long and endearing friendship.

God's design for us is that we work together, live together, and have fun together. When we choose to share our time and space with others, we will reap the rewards of joy and peace.

JOY

Thou hast put gladness in my heart, more than in the time that their corn and their wine increased.

Psalm 4:7 KJV

They that sow in tears shall reap in joy. He that goeth forth and weepeth, bearing precious seed, shall doubtless come again with rejoicing, bringing his sheaves with him.

Psalm 126:5-6 KJV

I will rejoice in the LORD, I will joy in the God of my salvation.

Habakkuk 3:18 KJV

Our heart shall rejoice in him, because we have trusted in his holy name.

Psalm 33:21 KJV

OVERFLOWING JOY

One day during her morning devotions, Jeannie found herself weeping as she read Psalm 139:23, "Search me, O God, and know my heart." She cried out to the Lord to cleanse her of several bad attitudes she had been harboring. Later that morning as she boarded an airplane, she had a strong feeling that God was confirming to her that He had forgiven her and could now use her for a special assignment. She whispered a prayer, "Lord, help me to stay awake."

Jeannie usually took motion-sickness medication before flying and, therefore, often slept from take-off to landing. On this flight, however, she forced herself to stay awake. A woman took the seat next to her on the flight, and as they began to talk, the woman asked, "Why do you have so much joy?"

Jeannie replied, "Because of Jesus." And for the next three hours, she had a wonderful opportunity to witness to the woman. Later, she sent her a Bible, and they exchanged letters. Then late one evening, the woman called, and Jeannie led her to the Lord over the phone.

The Lord will not only hear your heart's cry today, but His answer will fill you with overflowing joy that you will be able to share with others.

KNOWLEDGE

Praise God forever and ever, because he has wisdom and power. . . . He gives wisdom to those who are wise and knowledge to those who understand.

Daniel 2:20-21 NCV

104

Wisdom and knowledge will be the stability of your times, And the strength of salvation.

Isaiah 33:6 NKJV

O the depth of the riches both of the wisdom and knowledge of God! how unsearchable are his judgments, and his ways past finding out!

Romans 11:33 KJV

Wisdom will enter your heart And knowledge will be pleasant to your soul.

Proverbs 2:10 NASB

SUCCEED—READ!

After experiencing numerous failures in business and politics, Abraham Lincoln still maintained his daily habit of reading. A critic scoffed, "What good is all that education? It has never earned you a decent living."

Lincoln replied, "Education is not given for the purpose of earning a living; it's learning what to do with a living after you earn it that counts."

One of America's greatest reading advocates is Jim Trelease. He has devoted nearly two decades to promoting what he considers the most important social factor in our lives today. "The more you read," he says, "the smarter you grow. The smarter you grow, the longer you stay in school. The longer you stay in school, the more money you earn. The more you earn, the better your children will do in school. So if you hook a child with reading, you influence not only his future but also that of the next generation."

Reading researchers agree. They have long seen a correlation between the time people spend reading and the number of innovative ideas and creative solutions they have. Reading affects a person's ability to reason and communicate by providing an extended and accurate vocabulary.

Spend some time reading today. It will be time well spent because investing in your personal growth affects your future success.

KNOWLEDGE

A man of understanding and knowledge
maintains order.

Proverbs 28:2

The fear of the LORD is the beginning of wisdom,
and knowledge of the Holy One is understanding.

Proverbs 9:10

If I have the gift of prophecy and can fathom all
mysteries and all knowledge, and if I have a faith
that can move mountains, but have not love,
I am nothing.

1 Corinthians 13:2

Grow in the grace and knowledge of our Lord
and Savior Jesus Christ.

2 Peter 3:18 NASB

A "CAN-GET-IT-DONE" ATTITUDE

One Friday morning, an eager young student at Stanford University stood before Louis Janin. He was seeking part-time employment from Janin, who informed him, "All I need right now is a stenographer."

"Fine," the young man said eagerly, "I'll take the job." Then he added, "But I can't come back until Tuesday."

Janin agreed, and the next Tuesday, the young man reported for work as scheduled. Janin asked him, "Why is it that you couldn't come back before Tuesday?"

The young man replied, "Because I had to rent a typewriter and learn how to use it."

This zealous new typist was Herbert Hoover, whose "can-get-it-done" attitude eventually led him through the doors of the White House.

No skill you learn will ever be lost to you or prove to be of little use. If nothing more, the learning of new information and new skills builds confidence and exercises the mind. One of the secrets of great leaders is continuing education. Never quit learning! That's what gives you an edge over the competition.

LAUGHTER

There is a time for everything, and a season for every activity under heaven: . . . a time to weep and a time to laugh, a time to mourn and a time to dance.

Ecclesiastes 3:1,4

He will yet fill your mouth with laughter and your lips with shouts of joy.

Job 8:21

108

Our mouths were filled with laughter, our tongues with songs of joy.

Psalm 126:2

"Blessed are you who hunger now, for you will be satisfied. Blessed are you who weep now, for you will laugh."

Luke 6:21

WASHING WINDOWS

Ludwig Bemelmans wrote in *My War with the United States* that among the many regulations published by the U.S. Army is a book that gives advice on practical matters to noncommissioned officers. One piece of advice tells an officer how to help soldiers who have quarreled to become friends again. The men are to be assigned to wash the same window—one working on the outside, the other inside.

Says Bemelmans, "Looking at each other, they soon have to laugh, and all is forgotten. It works; I have tried it."

Laughter shared between friends is one of life's great treasures. Not only is laughter free, but it is a renewable resource and one with countless benefits. It restores a sense of balance to an oppressing day. It builds up energy in a flagging spirit. It helps lighten the load of sorrow, grief, and suffering. It tightens the bonds of relationships.

Laughter has an extremely high rate of return. It brings positive results when we are able to laugh with others.

LOSS

We know that in everything God works for good with those who love him, who are called according to his purpose.

Romans 8:28 RSV

I am convinced that nothing can ever separate us from his love. Death can't, and life can't. The angels can't, and the demons can't. Our fears for today, our worries about tomorrow, and even the powers of hell can't keep God's love away. Whether we are high above the sky or in the deepest ocean, nothing in all creation will ever be able to separate us from the love of God that is revealed in Christ Jesus our Lord.

Romans 8:38-39 NLT

If we live, we live to the Lord; and if we die, we die to the Lord. So, whether we live or die, we belong to the Lord.

Romans 14:8

The bodies we now have are weak and can die. But they will be changed into bodies that are eternal. Then the Scriptures will come true, "Death has lost the battle! Where is its victory? Where is its sting?"

1 Corinthians 15:54-55 CEV

THE SEEDS OF SUCCESS

On the night of December 9, 1914, Edison Industries was destroyed by fire. The loss exceeded $2 million and included the vast majority of Thomas Alva Edison's work. Edison was insured for only $238 because the buildings were constructed of concrete, which at that time, was thought to make a building fireproof. At sixty-seven years of age, Edison watched his life's work go up in flames.

The next morning, after firefighters had finally brought the inferno under control, Edison surveyed his charred dreams and crushed hopes. As he surveyed the scene, he said, "There is great value in disaster. All our mistakes are burned up. Thank God we can start anew."

Three weeks after the fire, Edison Industries produced the first phonograph.

In every setback, the seeds of a future success can be found if you are willing to look. And you may find that it is your most important success yet. Such a success, however, will not be automatic. The seeds of vision must be planted and fertilized with hope and hard work. Then they must be watered regularly with enthusiasm. Turn your trials into triumphs. It may be tough going for a while, but God is there to help you pull gold from the ashes.

LOSS

To all who mourn in Israel, he will give beauty
for ashes, joy instead of mourning, praise instead
of despair.

Isaiah 61:3 NLT

"Blessed are those who mourn, for they will
be comforted."

Matthew 5:4

112

As the sufferings of Christ abound in us, so our
consolation also abounds through Christ.

2 Corinthians 1:5 NKJV

Laugh with your happy friends when they're
happy; share tears when they're down.

Romans 12:15
THE MESSAGE

A THIRD-ACT TWIST

Comedienne Joan Rivers was devastated by the suicide of her husband and manager, Edgar Rosenberg. She describes working through her grief in her book, *Still Talking*. One of the things Rivers discovered during her experience was a deep inner strength. She writes:

What will I be doing in five years? I'm not worried—whether I am single, or married to a wonderful man. I'd love to be doing television, but nothing is secure in show business. Even if things go badly, the bottom I might hit would be nowhere near as deep as what I have been through. I have become my version of an optimist. If I can't get through one door, I'll go through another—or I'll make a door. Something terrific will come no matter how dark the present. God always comes up with a third-act twist. . . . That's the exhilaration of being alive. There is always another scene coming out of nowhere. God is the best dramatist.

When you are going through a crisis, it is often difficult to realize that you are doing just that—going through it. All crises are temporary! All storms eventually pass. Every night turns into a new morning. Choose to persist until you see the breaking of dawn!

LOVE

The fruit of the Spirit is love, joy, peace, long-suffering, gentleness, goodness, faith.

Galatians 5:22 KJV

Above all, love each other deeply, because love covers over a multitude of sins.

1 Peter 4:8

114

Whoever loves is a child of God and knows God. Whoever does not love does not know God, for God is love.

1 John 4:7-8 TEV

I have loved you with an everlasting love;
Therefore I have drawn you with lovingkindness.

Jeremiah 31:3 NASB

A WORTHY HERITAGE

When Everett Alvarez Jr. was given only thirty seconds to prepare a five-minute speech, he quickly thought back through his life. He recalled a time when he searched through his neighbor's trash for empty soda pop bottles to turn in at the corner grocery for a penny each.

All day, he carried bottles to the store in his red wagon until he had a small mountain of coins—just enough to buy a card and a candy bar. They were surprise birthday presents for his mother. When he returned home, his mother demanded, "Where have you been? I've been searching everywhere for you!"

As his mother continued her questioning, Ev blubbered through his tears, "I was collecting bottles to get you these." He handed her the unsigned card and the candy bar that had nearly snapped in two in his pocket. His mother then began to cry as she proudly placed the gifts on a window ledge so all the neighbors might see.

Ev's speech spoke to the hearts of his audience— a group of fellow prisoners of war, who had spent time at the infamous Hanoi Hilton prison camp in North Vietnam. For many of the men, it was the heritage of sacrificial family love that was their "suit of armor"—the "why" that enabled them to survive years of nightmarish torture.

LOVE

We need have no fear of someone who loves us perfectly; his perfect love for us eliminates all dread.

1 John 4:18 TLB

"Love your enemies, do good, and lend, hoping for nothing in return; and your reward will be great."

Luke 6:35 NKJV

116

"This is my commandment, That ye love one another, as I have loved you."

John 15:12 KJV

Those who do not love their brothers and sisters, whom they have seen, cannot love God, whom they have never seen.

1 John 4:20 NCV

THE POWER OF EMPATHY

In 1873, a Belgian Catholic priest named Joseph Damien De Veuster was sent to minister to lepers on the Hawaiian island of Molokai. He arrived in high spirits, hoping to build a friendship with each of the lepers. People shunned him, however, at every turn. He built a chapel, began worship services, poured his heart out to the lepers, but all seemed futile. No one responded to his ministry, and after twelve years of struggling, Father Damien decided to leave. As he stood in dejection on the dock waiting to board the ship, he looked down at the hands he was wringing and noticed some mysterious white spots on them. Feeling some numbness, he knew immediately what was happening—he had contracted leprosy!

Father Damien returned to the leper colony and to his work. Word spread quickly, and within hours, hundreds gathered outside his hut, fully identifying with his plight. A bigger surprise came the following Sunday. When he arrived at the chapel, he found it full! Father Damien began to preach from the empathy of love rather than the distance of theology and ideas, and his ministry became enormously successful.

Those who receive your love today will be much more interested in hearing about your faith tomorrow.

MONEY

The love of money is a root of all kinds of evil, for which some have strayed from the faith in their greediness, and pierced themselves through with many sorrows.

1 Timothy 6:10 NKJV

Give me an eagerness for your decrees; do not inflict me with love for money!

Psalm 119:36 NLT

118

Wisdom is a shelter as money is a shelter, but the advantage of knowledge is this: that wisdom preserves the life of its possessor.

Ecclesiastes 7:12

Instruct those who are rich in this present world not to be conceited or to fix their hope on the uncertainty of riches, but on God, who richly supplies us with all things to enjoy.

1 Timothy 6:17 NASB

MONEY, MONEY, MONEY

In 1923, eight of the most powerful money magnates in the world gathered for a meeting at the Edgewater Beach Hotel in Chicago, Illinois. The combined resources and assets of these eight men tallied more than the U.S. Treasury that year. In the group were the following men: Charles Schwab, president of a steel company; Richard Whitney, president of the New York Stock Exchange; Arthur Cutton, a wheat speculator; Albert Fall, a presidential cabinet member and personally wealthy man; Jesse Livermore, the greatest Wall Street "bear" in his generation; Leon Fraser, president of the International Bank of Settlements; and Ivan Krueger, head of the largest monopoly in the nation. What an impressive gathering of financial eagles!

What happened to these men in later years? Schwab died penniless. Whitney served a life sentence in Sing Sing prison. Cutton became insolvent. Fall was pardoned from a federal prison so that he might die at home. Fraser, Livermore, and Krueger committed suicide. Seven of these eight extremely rich men ended their lives with nothing.

Money is certainly not the answer to life's ills! Only God can give us peace, happiness, and joy. When we focus on God and His goodness, we can live contentedly, knowing that God will meet all our needs.

MONEY

"Don't store up treasures here on earth where they can erode away or may be stolen. Store them in heaven where they will never lose their value."

Matthew 6:19-20 TLB

Stay away from the love of money; be satisfied with what you have.

Hebrews 13:5 NLT

"Be careful and guard against all kinds of greed. Life is not measured by how much one owns."

Luke 12:15 NCV

"No one can serve two masters. Either he will hate the one and love the other, or he will be devoted to the one and despise the other. You cannot serve both God and Money."

Matthew 6:24

NEVER ENOUGH

A film editor once said, "I had this date the other night with a woman who wanted to walk along the beach. I'm wearing a twelve-hundred-dollar suit, a seventy-five-dollar tie, a hundred-and-fifty-dollar shirt, and a pair of two-hundred-dollar shoes. It costs me fifteen dollars to clean my suit and six dollars to have my shirt hand-washed.

"I don't even want to think about what it would cost if I should get a drop of spaghetti sauce on my tie. And this woman wants me to roll up my pants and walk along the beach! All I can think about is how much it's going to cost me if she wants to sit down on the sand. Here's the bottom line that I have to ask myself: *Can I afford to wear my own clothes?*"

Another man, a lawyer, once said, "I don't think I'm trapped on this treadmill forever, but I'm certainly involved with it right now. . . . It's the old merry-go-round of how much money is enough money? And it's never enough."[6]

Money should be a means toward living a generous, giving life—not an end in itself. When having money becomes your only goal, you may find yourself hoarding it and working too hard; then you will be unable to truly enjoy life.

OBEDIENCE

"Whosoever shall do the will of my Father which is in heaven, the same is my brother, and sister, and mother."

Matthew 12:50 KJV

Don't you know that when you offer yourselves to someone to obey him as slaves, you are slaves to the one whom you obey—whether you are slaves to sin, which leads to death, or to obedience, which leads to righteousness?

Romans 6:16

Samuel said, Hath the LORD as great delight in burnt offerings and sacrifices, as in obeying the voice of the LORD? Behold, to obey is better than sacrifice, and to hearken than the fat of rams.

1 Samuel 15:22 KJV

If they obey and serve him, they will spend the rest of their days in prosperity and their years in contentment.

Job 36:11

122

OBEDIENT CHOICES

In the eleventh century, King Henry III of Bavaria became tired of his responsibilities as king, the pressures of international politics, and the mundane worldliness of court life. He made an application to Prior Richard at a local monastery to be accepted as a contemplative and to spend the rest of his life in prayer and meditation there.

Prior Richard responded, "Your Majesty, do you understand that the pledge here is one of obedience? That will be hard for you since you have been a king."

"I understand," Henry said. "The rest of my life I will be obedient to you, as Christ leads you."

Prior Richard responded, "Then I will tell you what to do. Go back to your throne, and serve faithfully in the place where God has put you."

After King Henry died, this statement was written in his honor: "The king learned to rule by being obedient."

Each of us ultimately obeys either the righteous commandments of our Heavenly Father or the "rule of lawlessness." Wise leaders willingly choose to put themselves under authority, including the authority of God. They realize that if they fail to do so, they will have no law other than their own whim, an unreliable source at best!

OBEDIENCE

"He who has my commandments and keeps them,
he it is who loves me; and he who loves me will be
loved by my Father, and I will love him and
manifest myself to him."

John 14:21 RSV

124

Because of your obedience, the Lord your God
will keep his part of the contract which, in his
tender love, he made with your fathers.

Deuteronomy 7:12 TLB

When you obey me you are living in my love,
just as I obey my Father and live in his love.

John 15:10 TLB

If our consciences are clear, we can come to the
Lord with perfect assurance and trust, and get
whatever we ask for because we are obeying him
and doing the things that please him.

1 John 3:21-22 TLB

COMING CLEAN

Professional stock-car racer Darrell Waltrip was once proud of his image as "the guy folks loved to hate." Then things began to change. After miraculously surviving a crash in the Daytona 500, he began going to church with his wife, Stevie. They began trying to have a family but suffered four miscarriages.

One day their pastor came to visit. He asked, "Your car is sponsored by a beer company. Is that the image you want?" Darrell had never thought about it. He had always loved watching kids admire his car, but the more he thought about it, he discovered that he did care about his image. He thought, *If our prayers were answered for a child, what kind of dad would I be?*

He didn't know what to do to convince his car's owner to change sponsors, but amazingly, an opportunity opened for him to sign with a new racing team sponsored by a laundry detergent company! He switched teams. Two years later, daughter Jessica was born, and she was followed a few years later by daughter Sarah. In 1989, he won the Daytona.

Obedience to God and His Word opens the door for God to rain down blessings on our lives.

PATIENCE

Be patient and wait for the LORD to act; don't be
worried about those who prosper or those who
succeed in their evil plans.

Psalm 37:7 TEV

It is better to be patient than to be proud.
Don't become angry quickly, because getting
angry is foolish.

Ecclesiastes 7:8-9 NCV

When the Holy Spirit controls our lives he will
produce this kind of fruit in us: love, joy, peace,
patience, kindness, goodness, faithfulness.

Galatians 5:22 TLB

Be completely humble and gentle; be patient,
bearing with one another in love.

Ephesians 4:2

126

LEARNING TO WAIT

A young computer salesman named Kurt was delighted when one of his clients expressed interest in buying a used computer system—one that Kurt had installed two years ago but that had recently been replaced by an upgrade. After careful calculation and consultation with his home office, he fixed a price of $800,000 for the used system and documented all his reasons for requesting that amount.

As he sat down to negotiate, he heard an inner voice say, *Wait. Let them do the initial talking.* The buyers quickly filled the silence with a long rundown of their own research about this particular computer system's strengths and weaknesses, the age of the equipment, and the need for new software. "Can you throw upgraded software into the deal?" one of the buyers asked.

"Sure," Kurt offered.

The buyers then said, "We'll give you $950,000 for the system, but not a penny more."

Less than an hour later, the paperwork was signed, and Kurt walked away with a better deal than he had imagined, having said little more than, "Thank you."

Sometimes the best thing to say is nothing! Learning to wait requires patience and self-control, but it can pay big rewards as well.

PATIENCE

I waited patiently for the LORD to help me, and he turned to me and heard my cry.

Psalm 40:1 NLT

Let us lay aside every weight, and the sin which doth so easily beset us, and let us run with patience the race that is set before us.

Hebrews 12:1 KJV

Warn those who are unruly, comfort the fainthearted, uphold the weak, be patient with all.

1 Thessalonians 5:14 NKJV

A man's wisdom gives him patience.

Proverbs 19:11

IN A HURRY

A man's car once stalled in heavy Friday-evening traffic just as the light turned green. All his efforts to start the engine failed. A chorus of honking rose from the cars behind him.

Feeling just as frustrated as those other drivers who were eager to get home or to their weekend destinations, he finally got out of his car and walked back to the first driver and said, "I'm sorry, but I can't seem to get my car started. If you'll go up there and give it a try, I'll stay here and blow your horn for you."

The person who is chronically impatient rarely makes another person move more quickly or arrive any earlier. Rather, the effects are nearly always negative—to others as well as to the impatient person. Accidents occur more frequently in haste. Ulcers, headaches, and other health problems develop more quickly. And relationships can become more readily strained.

As an antidote for impatience, try giving yourself "ten more minutes." Get up ten minutes earlier every morning, leave your home ten minutes earlier, arrive ten minutes ahead of schedule, and so forth. You'll likely arrive at the end of the day feeling much more relaxed.

PEACE

Great peace have they who love your law, and
nothing can make them stumble.

Psalm 119:165

LORD, You will establish peace for us,
Since You have also performed for us all our works.

Isaiah 26:12 NASB

130

Be perfect, be of good comfort, be of one mind,
live in peace; and the God of love and peace shall
be with you.

2 Corinthians 13:11 KJV

When a man's ways are pleasing to the LORD,
He makes even his enemies to be at peace
with him.

Proverbs 16:7 NASB

PERFECT STILLNESS

Joni Eareckson-Tada has written the following in *Decision* magazine:

A large part of me never moves, because I'm paralyzed from the shoulders down. It's like instant stillness! I don't run, I sit. I don't race, I wait. . . . My "natural" stillness used to drive me crazy. After my diving injury, I lay still for three months waiting to be moved from the intensive care unit into a regular hospital room. . . . While in rehab, I stayed put in my wheelchair for hours outside physical therapy and in the evenings my stillness would madden me as I sat by the door waiting for friends or family to come for a visit. It was more frightening at night when I lay down . . . at least in my wheelchair I could flail my arms and shrug my shoulders, but in bed I couldn't move at all except to turn my head on the pillow. My bed was an altar of affliction. But time, prayer and study in God's Word have a way of changing things. Now, many years later, my bed is an altar of praise. It's the one spot where I always meet God in total, relaxed stillness. In fact, as soon as I wheel into my bedroom and see the side lamp lit, it signals in my mind: "It's time to be still and to know more about God . . . it's time to pray."[7]

Find a quiet place where you can sit in the presence of God each day. During this time, let Him fill you with His peace and give you the strength you need to face the day.

PEACE

Turn your back on sin; do something good.
Embrace peace—don't let it get away!

Psalm 34:14 THE MESSAGE

Since we have been made right in God's sight by
faith, we have peace with God because of what
Jesus Christ our Lord has done for us.

Romans 5:1 NLT

132

May the God of hope fill you with all joy and
peace as you trust in him, so that you may overflow
with hope by the power of the Holy Spirit.

Romans 15:13

The meek shall inherit the earth; and shall delight
themselves in the abundance of peace.

Psalm 37:11 KJV

SOWING PEACE

When Abraham Lincoln was campaigning for the presidency, one of his archenemies was Edwin McMasters Stanton. Stanton hated Lincoln and used every ounce of his energy to degrade Lincoln in the eyes of the public, often using the bitterest diatribes in an attempt to embarrass him.

In the process of choosing his cabinet after his election, Lincoln selected various members and then faced a decision about the important post of Secretary of War. After careful consideration, he chose Stanton! The president's inner circle erupted in an uproar when they heard his choice. Numerous advisors came to Lincoln saying, "Mr. President, you are making a mistake. Are you familiar with all the ugly things he has said about you? He is your enemy. He will sabotage your programs."

Lincoln replied, "Yes, I know Mr. Stanton. But . . . I find he is the best man for the job." His inner peace gave him the confidence to overrule an affront to his own ego and do the right thing.

As Secretary of War, Stanton gave invaluable service to his nation and his president. After Lincoln was assassinated, many laudable statements were made about Abraham Lincoln, but the words of Stanton remain among the greatest. Standing near Lincoln's coffin, Stanton called Lincoln one of the greatest men who ever lived and said, "He now belongs to the ages."

PERSEVERANCE

Consider it pure joy, my brothers, whenever you face trials of many kinds, because you know that the testing of your faith develops perseverance. Perseverance must finish its work so that you may be mature and complete, not lacking anything.
James 1:2-4

134 May the Master take you by the hand and lead you along the path of God's love and Christ's endurance.
2 Thessalonians 3:5
THE MESSAGE

Love bears up under anything *and* everything that comes, is ever ready to believe the best of every person, its hopes are fadeless under all circumstances, and it endures everything [without weakening].
1 Corinthians 13:7 AMP

If anyone suffers as a Christian, he is not to be ashamed, but is to glorify God in His name.
1 Peter 4:16 NASB

WRONG ADDRESS

Mr. Boswell, the owner of a hardware store, was looking for a young man to hire. Several dozen young men responded to his ad, but he eventually narrowed his choice to three: Ted, John, and Bob. Then he devised a final test. He gave each of them a new screwdriver set with an innovative design and told them to deliver it to Mr. C. M. Henderson at 314 Maple Street.

After a while, Ted phoned the store to ask whether the number was actually 413, rather than 314. Later, he returned saying there was no house at that address.

When John came back, he reported that 314 Maple was a funeral parlor and that Mr. Henderson had lived at 314 ½, but had moved away.

Bob took longer than the other two young men. Like John, he also discovered that Mr. Henderson had moved away, but he had managed to secure his new address and had gone there. Mr. Henderson didn't recall ordering the screwdriver, but when Bob pointed out its unique features and told him the price, Mr. Henderson decided he wanted the screwdriver and paid for it on the spot.

Which young man was hired? Bob, of course. He was given a task to do, and he did it. True leaders don't let any obstacles stop them from reaching their goals. Persistence and patience produce payoff.

PERSEVERANCE

We also glory in tribulations, knowing that
tribulation produces perseverance; and
perseverance, character; and character, hope.

Romans 5:3-4 NKJV

You need to persevere so that when you have
done the will of God, you will receive what
he has promised.

Hebrews 10:36

"The good soil represents honest, good-hearted
people who hear God's message, cling to it, and
steadily produce a huge harvest."

Luke 8:15 NLT

Pray at all times in the Spirit, with all prayer and
supplication. To that end keep alert with all
perseverance, making supplication for all the saints.

Ephesians 6:18 RSV

SAVING FOR A DREAM

After his parents were brutally murdered in North Vietnam, Ri moved to South Vietnam, where he went to school and eventually became a building contractor. Ri prospered greatly until he was arrested while on a trip north. After being imprisoned in North Vietnam for three years, he finally escaped and made his way south, only to be charged as a spy for the north!

When he learned that the United States was pulling out of South Vietnam, he gave all his worldly possessions in exchange for passage on a small, overcrowded fishing boat. He was later rescued by an American ship and taken to the Philippines, where he lived in a refugee camp for two years.

Finally he was released to the United States, where Ri's cousin offered both him and his wife jobs in his tailor shop. Their net pay was only $300 a week, but they were able to save by living in the back room of the tailor shop and taking sponge baths. Within two years, they had saved enough to buy out the cousin's business. It was only then that they rented an apartment.

Today, Ri is a millionaire. Hard work and frugal living can bring a dream into reality! A leader is not leading if he or she is not moving forward.

PRAYER

"When you pray, go away by yourself, all alone, and shut the door behind you and pray to your Father secretly, and your Father, who knows your secrets, will reward you."

Matthew 6:6 TLB

138

Even before they finish praying to me, I will answer their prayers.

Isaiah 65:24 TEV

"Believe that you have received the things you ask for in prayer, and God will give them to you."

Mark 11:24 NCV

The earnest prayer of a righteous person has great power and wonderful results.

James 5:16 NLT

UNCHANGING FAITHFULNESS

I n the introduction to Catherine Marshall's *A Closer Walk*, her husband of twenty-three years, Leonard LeSourd, writes about their marriage in 1959:

> Catherine had huge adjustments to make. She sold her Washington dream house to move to Chappaqua, forty miles north of New York City, so that I could continue to commute to my job at Guideposts in the city. My children—Linda, ten; Chester, six; Jeffry, three—had been through a deeply unsettling two years, adjusting to a variety of housekeepers. They had mixed feelings toward moving into a new house, and especially toward "the new Mommie that Daddy's bringing home." Catherine's son, Peter John, nineteen, was going through a period of rebellion at Yale. Catherine and I had so many things to pray about that we began to rise an hour early each morning to read the Bible and seek answers together. Her current journal lay open beside us in these pre-dawn prayer times, recording our changing needs, His unchanging faithfulness.[8]

It's a simple fact of life that the more you have crammed into your schedule and the more problems you have, the more you have to pray about! Remember to turn to God in prayer; He is always there waiting to give you the strength and encouragement you need.

PRAYER

The eyes of the Lord watch over those who do right, and his ears are open to their prayers.

1 Peter 3:12 NLT

"When you are praying, if you are angry with someone, forgive him so that your Father in heaven will also forgive your sins."

Mark 11:25 NCV

Call unto me, and I will answer thee, and shew thee great and mighty things, which thou knowest not.

Jeremiah 33:3 KJV

When good people pray, the LORD listens.

Proverbs 15:29 TEV

THE HABIT OF PRAYER

A surgeon in a large city hospital had a habit of insisting on a few minutes alone before he performed an operation. He had an outstanding reputation as a surgeon, and one of the young doctors who often worked with him wondered if there might be a correlation between his unusual habit and his unprecedented success.

To the young doctor's inquiry, the surgeon answered, "Yes, there's a relationship. Before each operation, I ask the Great Physician to be with me, to guide my hands in their work. There have been times when I didn't know what to do next in a surgery, and then came the power to go on—power I knew came from God. I would not think of performing an operation without asking for His help."

The surgeon's words quickly spread through the hospital and then across the country. One day a father brought his daughter to the hospital, insisting that the only doctor he would allow to touch her was the one who worked with God.

One of the greatest elements you can put into your work hours, regardless of your field, is prayer. Take some time to cover your work in prayer, and He will help you to achieve more.

PRIDE

To fear the LORD is to hate evil; I hate pride and arrogance, evil behavior and perverse speech.

Proverbs 8:13

"Everyone who exalts himself will be humbled, and he who humbles himself will be exalted."

Luke 18:14 NKJV

142

A man's pride will bring him low,
But a humble spirit will obtain honor.

Proverbs 29:23 NASB

Pride leads to arguments; be humble, take advice and become wise.

Proverbs 13:10 TLB

YIELD YOUR PRIDE

While driving down a country road, a man came to a narrow bridge. In front of the bridge was a sign that read, "Yield." Seeing no oncoming cars, the man continued across the bridge and on to his destination. On his way back along this same route, the man came to the same one-lane bridge from the opposite direction. To his surprise, he saw another "Yield" sign posted there.

Curious, he thought. *I'm sure there was a sign posted on the other side.* Sure enough, when he reached the other side of the bridge and looked back, he saw the sign. Yield signs had been placed at both ends of the bridge so that the drivers from both directions would give each other the right of way. It appeared to be a reasonable way to prevent a head-on collision.

If you find yourself in a combative situation with someone else, don't let your pride keep you from yielding. If they have more authority than you, your lack of submission will put you in a bad position. If you are of equal authority, an exercise of your power will only build resentment in a person better kept as an ally. In either circumstance, a wise leader recognizes that the best way to avoid a collision is to yield.

PRIDE

The patient in spirit is better than the proud in spirit.

Ecclesiastes 7:8 NKJV

Pride will destroy a person; a proud attitude leads to ruin.

Proverbs 16:18 NCV

144

Do not think of yourself more highly than you should. Instead, be modest in your thinking.

Romans 12:3 TEV

When pride comes, then comes disgrace, but with humility comes wisdom.

Proverbs 11:2

A TRUTHFUL TALE

The story is told of an old minister who survived the great Johnstown flood. He loved to tell the story over and over, usually in great detail. Everywhere he went, all he talked about was this great historic event in his life. Eventually, the minister died and went to Heaven.

In Heaven, he attended a meeting of saints who had gathered to share their life experiences. The minister was very excited, and he ran to ask Peter if he might relate the incredible story of his survival from the Johnstown flood.

Peter hesitated for a moment and then said, "Yes, you may share, but just remember that Noah will be in the audience tonight."

When you tell the tales of your life, it is always wise to remember that there may be people hidden somewhere in your audience who will know if what you say is true and accurate or merely a prideful boast. Those people might have been eyewitnesses to the event, or they may have had a similar experience but on a much greater scale.

The best course is always to tell your experience as accurately as possible. Both understatements and exaggerations are prideful lies that should be avoided, especially by leaders.

PRIORITIES

Trust in the LORD with all your heart; do not depend on your own understanding. Seek his will in all you do, and he will direct your paths.

Proverbs 3:5-6 NLT

The LORD has told us what is good. What he requires of us is this: to do what is just, to show constant love, and to live in humble fellowship with our God.

Micah 6:8 TEV

146

This is what the LORD says: "Stand at the crossroads and look; ask for the ancient paths, ask where the good way is, and walk in it, and you will find rest for your souls."

Jeremiah 6:16

Saul prayed to the LORD, the God of Israel, "Give me the right answer."

1 Samuel 14:41

ONE TO SIX

Charles Schwab, one of the first presidents of Bethlehem Steel, once asked an efficiency expert to help him be more productive at work. The efficiency expert told Schwab he could increase Schwab's productivity by at least 50 percent with a simple system. He then handed Schwab a piece of paper and instructed him to write down the six most important tasks he would have to do the next day and number them in the order of their importance.

Then the man said, "Put this paper in your pocket. First thing tomorrow morning, look at the first item, and start working on it until it is finished. Then tackle the next item in the same way, and so on. Do this until quitting time every working day. After you've tried this system for a while, have your men try it. Then send me a check for what you think it's worth."

A few weeks later Schwab sent the expert a check for $25,000, calling his advice the most profitable lesson he had ever learned. And in just five years, largely by following this simple system, Bethlehem Steel became the largest independent steel producer in the world.

What are the six most important tasks you have to do tomorrow? Write them down, and purpose in your heart to accomplish them!

PRIORITIES

"The more lowly your service to others, the greater you are. To be the greatest, be a servant."
Matthew 23:11 TLB

Respect the LORD your God, and do what he has told you to do. Love him. Serve the LORD your God with your whole being, and obey the LORD's commands and laws.
Deuteronomy 10:12-13 NCV

148

Decide today whom you will obey. . . . As for me and my family, we will serve the Lord.
Joshua 24:15 TLB

"He will give you all you need from day to day if you live for him and make the Kingdom of God your primary concern."
Matthew 6:33 NLT

REALIGNED PRIORITIES

Colonel Rahl, the Hessian commander at Trenton, was in the middle of a game of cards when a courier brought a message to him. Rahl casually put the letter in his pocket, but he did not read it until the game was finished. When he finally opened the note, he read that Washington was crossing the Delaware River. Rahl quickly rallied his men, but he was too late. He died just before his regiment was taken captive. Because of misplaced priorities, he lost honor, liberty, and his life.

Many a potential success has been thwarted because of misplaced priorities and unexecuted resolutions. In evaluating your immediate future and your ultimate goals, ask yourself these questions:

1. What do I hope to achieve in my life? What is my motivation for accomplishing these goals? Are my actions helping me attain my goals?

2. Is this what God requires of me? Given the talents, traits, experiences, and abilities He has given me, does it seem likely that this is what God has prepared for me to do and desires that I accomplish for His sake?

If your answer to this second question is no, then your priorities need to be realigned. If your answer is yes, then do what you know to do with as much energy and enthusiasm as possible!

PROTECTION

You have done so much for those who come
to you for protection.

Psalm 31:19 NLT

When you pass through the waters, I will be with
you; And through the rivers, they will not overflow
you. When you walk through the fire, you will not
be scorched, Nor will the flame burn you.

Isaiah 43:2 NASB

The eyes of the LORD run to and fro throughout
the whole earth, to show Himself strong on behalf
of those whose heart is loyal to Him.

2 Chronicles 16:9 NKJV

The Lord is faithful, and he will strengthen and
protect you from the evil one.

2 Thessalonians 3:3

NO "IFS"

n *The Hiding Place,* Corrie ten Boom writes about the tense times her family experienced in Holland during the German invasion. One night, as Corrie tossed restlessly on her bed while war bombers droned overhead and artillery burst nearby, she heard her sister downstairs in the kitchen.

Unable to sleep, she arose and joined Betsie for a cup of tea. The two talked well into the night until the sound of the bombers died away. They knew that explosions had ripped an area nearby, but all had become quiet.

As Corrie stumbled through the darkness back to her room, she reached down to pat her pillow before laying down. As she did, something sharp cut her hand. It turned out to be a ten-inch-long piece of jagged metal! She cried out for her sister and raced back down the stairs, holding the shrapnel in her hand.

As Betsie bandaged her hand, she said repeatedly, "On your pillow!"

Corrie said, "Betsie, if I hadn't heard you in the kitchen. . . ."

To this her sister firmly said, "Don't say it, Corrie! There are no 'ifs' in God's world. The center of His will is our safety."

Corrie later took that message around the world: "God's will is our hiding place."

PROTECTION

He orders his angels to protect you wherever
you go.

Psalm 91:11 NLT

The LORD thy God in the midst of thee is mighty;
he will save, he will rejoice over thee with joy.

Zephaniah 3:17 KJV

152

He protects those who are loyal to him, but evil
people will be silenced in darkness. Power is not
the key to success.

1 Samuel 2:9 NCV

Let all who take refuge in you be glad; let them
ever sing for joy. Spread your protection over them,
that those who love your name may rejoice in you.

Psalm 5:11

TRUE RICHES

One day the Reverend John Newton called upon a Christian family who had suffered the loss of all they possessed in a devastating fire. He greeted the wife and mother of the family by saying, "I give you joy."

The woman seemed surprised at his words—almost offended—and replied, "What! Joy that all my property is consumed?"

"Oh, no," Newton answered, "but joy that you have so much property that fire cannot touch."

His words reminded her of the true riches of her life—those things that she valued beyond measure: her husband, whom she loved very much; her children, the light of her life; the good health that they all possessed; their joy in each other; their faith in God; the love of friends and an extended family; and their prayers for a future together.

153

None of these riches can be bought, bargained for, or appraised. They come from within the heart and in the joy and peace of mind that comes from our belief in Jesus Christ. Surely it was His hand that brought her family safely through their ordeal.[9]

READING THE BIBLE

The whole Bible was given to us by inspiration from God and is useful to teach us what is true and to make us realize what is wrong in our lives.

2 Timothy 3:16 TLB

The word of God is alive and active, sharper than any double-edged sword. It cuts all the way through, to where soul and spirit meet. . . . It judges the desires and thoughts of the heart.

Hebrews 4:12 TEV

154

Your word is a lamp to my feet And a light to my path.

Psalm 119:105 NKJV

Do not let this Book of the Law depart from your mouth; meditate on it day and night, so that you may be careful to do everything written in it. Then you will be prosperous and successful.

Joshua 1:8

ROOTED IN GOD

Psalm 1 describes two ways to view and experience life. One approach is scornful, negative, pessimistic, and cynical. The psalmist says those who live this way have shallow roots and will wither when a dry season comes because they have no true source of nourishment in their lives.

The other approach to life accepts the things of God and results in a life that is happy, principled, well grounded, and delightful. The people who follow this way are likened to trees planted near steadily flowing streams. Their roots go deep and are always supplied with life-giving water even in times of trouble or drought.

The Bible clearly says that those who leave God out of their lives will not have staying power. Nothing will truly satisfy them. Nothing will seem worthwhile. Yet those who embrace God and the things of God will produce, multiply, and create things of lasting value for themselves and others.

Evaluate your life today. Are you satisfied with its direction? How deep are your roots in God's soil? Are you planted beside His life-giving stream? If you wish to find true satisfaction, let the Bible's words shape your lifestyle.

READING THE BIBLE

So shall My word be that goes forth from
My mouth; It shall not return to Me void,
But it shall accomplish what I please,
And it shall prosper in the thing for which I sent it.
Isaiah 55:11 NKJV

156

Study to shew thyself approved unto God, a
workman that needeth not to be ashamed, rightly
dividing the word of truth.
2 Timothy 2:15 KJV

I have not neglected your instructions, because
you yourself are my teacher.
Psalm 119:102 TEV

The teachings of the LORD are perfect; they give
new strength. The rules of the LORD can be
trusted; they make plain people wise.
Psalm 19:7 NCV

A LASTING LEGACY

Abraham Lincoln is often heralded as the greatest American president. His spirituality was undoubtedly the greatest reason for the decisions that led to his success, and he repeatedly referred to his indebtedness to and regard for the Bible.

Lincoln began reading the Bible in his boyhood. Its influence upon him increased over the years. Whenever he addressed the public, he quoted from the Bible more than from any other book. Lincoln's literary style mirrored the style of the Bible, especially the writings of the prophets of Israel. His deeply moving second inaugural speech is strongly reminiscent of the book of Isaiah. Lincoln also thought in terms of biblical ideas and convictions to an extent that has been unparalleled among modern statesmen.

Moreover, Lincoln was a man of prayer. Without apology or self-consciousness, Lincoln did not hesitate to request the prayers of others or to acknowledge that he himself prayed often. He regarded prayer as a necessity and routinely spoke of seeking divine guidance as though it was an entirely natural and reasonable thing to do.

Never curtail your pursuit of God. Never stop reading God's Word. It is the most important thing you can do to leave a lasting legacy of accomplishment, purpose, and true leadership.

SELF-CONTROL

Those who belong to Christ Jesus have nailed the passions and desires of their sinful nature to his cross.

Galatians 5:24 NLT

How can a young person live a pure life? By obeying your word.

Psalm 119:9 NCV

158

Set a watch, O LORD, before my mouth; keep the door of my lips. Incline not my heart to any evil thing.

Psalm 141:3-4 KJV

I urge you, brethren, by the mercies of God, to present your bodies a living and holy sacrifice, acceptable to God, which is your spiritual service of worship.

Romans 12:1 NASB

TAKE IT IN STRIDE

Astronaut Shannon Lucid was not supposed to set an American record for time spent in space. However, her assignment was extended because of technical difficulties with shuttle booster rockets and adverse weather conditions. Lucid ultimately stayed in space 188 days, setting a United States space endurance record and a world record for a female astronaut.

What many reports failed to note in the wake of Lucid's record-setting stay on the Russian space station *Mir* was the excellent reputation that Lucid had with her Russian hosts. This reputation was based not only on her technical expertise as an astronaut but also on the fact that her Russian counterparts never once heard her complain during her six-month stay. Every time Lucid was notified of a shuttle delay, she took the news in stride.

Valery Ryumin, a Russian space manager, noted that Lucid reacted like Russian cosmonauts do when their missions are extended. Ryumin said that Russia deliberately chooses cosmonauts "who are strong enough not to show any feelings" when they receive bad news.

Complaining not only makes you feel negative, but it spreads your negativity to others. True leaders will attempt to turn unpleasant or disappointing situations into positive ones by exercising self-control, maintaining a good attitude, and speaking uplifting words.

SELF-CONTROL

Do not let any unwholesome talk come out of your mouths, but only what is helpful for building others up according to their needs, that it may benefit those who listen.

Ephesians 4:29

160

Follow the Lord's rules for doing his work, just as an athlete either follows the rules or is disqualified and wins no prize.

2 Timothy 2:5 TLB

Knowing God leads to self-control. Self-control leads to patient endurance, and patient endurance leads to godliness.

2 Peter 1:6 NLT

Clothe yourselves with the Lord Jesus Christ, and do not think about how to gratify the desires of the sinful nature.

Romans 13:14

KEEP YOUR SHIRT ON

In the 1950s, President Truman appointed Newbold Morris to investigate allegations of crime and mismanagement in high levels of government. A few months later, Morris was himself in the witness chair in the Senate hearing room, answering a barrage of questions from a subcommittee about the sale of some ships by his New York company.

The investigation was intense. The subcommittee's questions were becoming increasingly accusatory. Morris's face first recorded pain, then surprise, and finally anger. Amidst a flurry of irate murmurs in the room, he rose, reached into his coat, and produced a sheet of white paper. Then he shouted: "Wait a minute. I have a note here from my wife. It says, 'Keep your shirt on!'"

Everyone in the room burst into laughter, and the angry situation was temporarily diffused.

Anger that is allowed to rage on eventually plays out in one of two ways: abuse or estrangement. Abuse—both physical blows and emotional wounds—and estrangement are painful situations. Reconciliation can be very difficult, and the healing process is often a long one. How much better it is to control yourself and your anger. Channel the intense feelings of rage into positive, productive expenditures of energy, and whenever possible, lighten the moment.

SELF-DISCIPLINE

Do not give in to bodily passions, which are
always at war against the soul.

1 Peter 2:11 TEV

Everything in the world—the cravings of sinful
man, the lust of his eyes and the boasting of what
he has and does—comes not from the Father
but from the world.

1 John 2:16

Let my heart be blameless regarding Your statutes,
That I may not be ashamed.

Psalm 119:80 NKJV

Those who belong to Christ Jesus have crucified
their own sinful selves. They have given up their
old selfish feelings and the evil things they
wanted to do.

Galatians 5:24 NCV

GIVE YOURSELF A CHECKUP

A young boy walked into a drugstore one day and asked to use the telephone. He dialed a number and said, "Hello, Dr. Anderson, do you want to hire a boy to cut your grass and run errands for you?" After a pause he said, "Oh, you already have a boy? Are you completely satisfied with the job he's doing?" Another pause. "All right then, good-bye, Doctor."

As the boy thanked the druggist and prepared to leave, the druggist called to him. "Just a minute, son. I couldn't help but overhear your conversation. If you are looking for work, I could use a boy like you."

"Thank you, sir," the boy replied, "but I already have a job."

"You do?" the druggist responded. "But didn't you just try to get a job from Dr. Anderson?"

"No, sir," the boy said. "I already work for Dr. Anderson. I was just checking up on myself."

A self-disciplined individual looks for ways to improve performance and avoid mistakes. Ask those with whom and for whom you work to give you suggestions on how you might do better, achieve more, and grow to the next level. When you check up on yourself, others won't feel it necessary to do so!

SELF-DISCIPLINE

God did not give us a spirit of timidity, but a spirit
of power, of love and of self-discipline.
2 Timothy 1:7

I advise you to obey only the Holy Spirit's
instructions. He will tell you where to go and
what to do, and then you won't always be doing
the wrong things your evil nature wants you to.
Galatians 5:16 TLB

164

Control yourselves and be careful! The devil, your
enemy, goes around like a roaring lion looking for
someone to eat. Refuse to give in to him, by
standing strong in your faith.
1 Peter 5:8-9 NCV

Let the Lord Jesus Christ take control of you, and
don't think of ways to indulge your evil desires.
Romans 13:14 NLT

YOU CAN FLY

Michael Stone had always dreamed of flying. A young man of extreme dedication and discipline, Michael chose to pursue the "flying" of pole vaulting. At age fourteen, he began a regimented program to achieve his goal. He worked out every other day with weights, and on alternate days, he ran. Michael's father, his coach and trainer, monitored the program. Besides being an athlete, Michael was also an honor-roll student, and he helped his parents with their farm.

At age seventeen, Michael faced his greatest athletic challenge. People watched as the pole was set at 17 feet—several inches higher than Michael's personal best. He cleared it, and then he cleared the pole at 17 feet 2 inches and again at 17 feet 4 inches.

In his final vault, Michael needed to fly 9 inches higher than he ever had before. Taking deep breaths to relax, he sprinted down the runway to an effortless takeoff. Michael began to fly and cleared the bar, setting a new National and International Junior Olympics record. His years of practice and self-discipline in pursuit of a goal had resulted in victory, one made even sweeter by the fact that Michael Stone is blind.

Choose to endure today in the pursuit of your goals; with self-discipline, they are within reach!

SHAME

Fear not; you will no longer live in shame.
The shame of your youth . . . will be
remembered no more.

Isaiah 54:4 TLB

No one whose hope is in you will ever be put
to shame, but they will be put to shame who
are treacherous without excuse.

Psalm 25:3

166

May those who hope in you not be disgraced
because of me, O Lord, the LORD Almighty;
may those who seek you not be put to shame.

Psalm 69:6

See, I lay in Zion a stone that causes men to
stumble and a rock that makes them fall, and the
one who trusts in him will never be put to shame.

Romans 9:33

DOWN IN THE MIRE

D. L. Moody told the story of a Chinese convert who gave this testimony:

I was down in a deep pit crying for someone to help me out. As I looked up, I saw a gray-haired man looking down at me. I said, "Can you help me out?" "My son," he replied, "I am Confucius. If you had read my books and followed what I taught, you would never have fallen into this dreadful pit." Then he was gone.

Soon I saw another man coming. "My son," Buddha said, "forget about yourself. Get into a state of rest. Then, my child, you will be in a delicious state just as I am." "Yes," I said, "I will do that when I am above this mire. Can you help me out?" I looked, and he was gone.

I was beginning to sink into despair when I saw another figure above me. There were marks of suffering on His face. "My child," He said, "what is the matter?" But before I could reply, He was down in the mire by my side. He folded His arms about me and lifted. He did not say, "Shame on you for falling into that pit." Instead He said, "We will walk on together now."

Wise leaders freely give all of their problems to God, knowing that He will not let them be put to shame. They allow Him to move on their behalf, and they are rewarded for their trust.

SHAME

Do your best to present yourself to God as one approved, a workman who does not need to be ashamed and who correctly handles the word of truth.

2 Timothy 2:15

We are able to hold our heads high no matter what happens and know that all is well, for we know how dearly God loves us, and we feel this warm love everywhere within us because God has given us the Holy Spirit to fill our hearts with his love.

Romans 5:5 TLB

Being justified by faith, we have peace with God through our Lord Jesus Christ.

Romans 5:1 KJV

We have renounced secret and shameful ways; we do not use deception, nor do we distort the word of God. On the contrary, by setting forth the truth plainly we commend ourselves to every man's conscience in the sight of God.

2 Corinthians 4:2

THE PARTS OF A SUCCESSFUL LIFE

Wallace E. Johnson, president of Holiday Inns and one of America's most successful builders, once said:

I always keep on a card in my billfold the following verses and refer to them frequently: "Ask, and it shall be given you; seek, and ye shall find; knock, and it shall be opened unto you: For every one that asketh receiveth; and he that seeketh findeth; and to him that knocketh it shall be opened" (Matthew 7:7-8 KJV).

These verses are among God's greatest promises. Yet they are a little one-sided. They indicate a philosophy of receiving, but not of giving. One day as my wife, Alma, and I were seeking God's guidance for a personal problem, I came across the following verse which has since been a daily reminder to me of what my responsibility as a businessman is to God: "Study to shew thyself approved unto God, a workman that needeth not to be ashamed, rightly dividing the word of truth" (2 Timothy 2:15 KJV).

Since then I have measured my actions against the phrase: "A workman that needeth not to be ashamed."

As a leader, what standard do you measure your actions against?

SPEECH

Let your speech always be gracious, seasoned
with salt, so that you may know how you ought
to answer every one.

Colossians 4:6 RSV

The mouth of the righteous man utters wisdom,
and his tongue speaks what is just.

Psalm 37:30

170

Whoso keepeth his mouth and his tongue
keepeth his soul from troubles.

Proverbs 21:23 KJV

You must understand this, my beloved: let everyone
be quick to listen, slow to speak, slow to anger.

James 1:19 NRSV

DON'T QUOTE ME

President Calvin Coolidge, the thirtieth president of the United States, was a reserved man with a dry sense of humor. He was also known for the fact that he spoke very little. A reporter once attempted to interview him, and the conversation went as follows:

Reporter: Do you wish to say anything about the war threat in Europe?

Coolidge: No.

Reporter: About the strike in the clothing factories?

Coolidge: No.

Reporter: About the League of Nations?

Coolidge: No.

Reporter: About the farm production problem?

Coolidge: No.

As the reporter rose and walked toward the door, Coolidge unexpectedly called back to him and said, "Don't quote me."

Never let yourself feel pressured into saying something you don't want to say or saying something when you don't feel like talking. Silence is not a "lack" of communication. It is a form of communication, and it can be a very effective one at that. Measure your words carefully, and be sure to say what you mean and mean what you say. This rule is especially important for leaders.

SPEECH

A soft answer turns away wrath, but a harsh word stirs up anger.

Proverbs 15:1 NRSV

The tongue can no man tame; it is an unruly evil, full of deadly poison.

James 3:8 KJV

172

How great a forest is set ablaze by a small fire! And the tongue is a fire.

James 3:5-6 NRSV

Let the words of my mouth, and the meditation of my heart, be acceptable in thy sight, O LORD, my strength, and my redeemer.

Psalm 19:14 KJV

POWERFUL WORDS

One day, a young altar boy was serving the priest at a Sunday Mass being held in the country church of his small village. The boy, nervous in his new role at the altar, accidentally dropped the cruet of wine. The village priest immediately struck the boy sharply on the cheek and in a very gruff voice, shouted so that many people could hear, "Leave the altar and don't come back!" That boy became Tito, the Communist leader who ruled Yugoslavia for many decades.

One day in a large city cathedral, a young boy was serving a bishop at a Sunday Mass. He, too, accidentally dropped the cruet of wine. The bishop turned to him, but rather than responding in anger, he gently whispered with a warm twinkle in his eyes, "Someday you will be a priest." That boy grew up to become Archbishop Fulton Sheen.

Words have power. The childhood phrase, "Sticks and stones can break my bones, but words can never hurt me" simply isn't true. Words can hurt. They wound—sometimes deeply.

But words can also reward, build self-esteem, create friendships, give hope, and render a blessing. Words can heal and drive accomplishment. Watch what you say today! Your words can produce life or death.

SPIRITUAL GROWTH

LET US STOP going over the same old ground again
and again, always teaching those first lessons about
Christ. Let us go on instead to other things and
become mature in our understanding, as strong
Christians ought to be.

Hebrews 6:1 TLB

174

Practice these things and devote yourself to them,
in order that your progress may be seen by all.

1 Timothy 4:15 TEV

Study to shew thyself approved unto God,
a workman that needeth not to be ashamed,
rightly dividing the word of truth.

2 Timothy 2:15 KJV

Open my eyes to see the wonderful truths in
your law.

Psalm 119:18 NLT

THE MEASURE OF A MAN

Most of us come to the lofty opinion we have of ourselves by means of comparison. In our judgment of others, we conclude, "I'm not like that person. I'm superior to those people." Pride does not exist in a vacuum. In the process of raising ourselves up "on a pedestal," we inevitably leave others in the dust.

A poem by an unknown author addresses this sorry attribute of mankind in a clever way:

> I dreamed death came the other night;
> And heaven's gates swung wide.
> With kindly grace an angel
> Ushered me inside.

> And there, to my astonishment,
> Stood folks I'd known on earth.
> Some I'd judged and labeled
> Unfit or of little worth.

> Indignant words rose to my lips,
> But never were set free;
> For every face showed stunned surprise—
> No one expected me!

Rather than measuring yourself against other people, measure yourself against your own potential. When you use this standard, you will always be able to reach farther and dream bigger.

SPIRITUAL GROWTH

Put on all of God's armor so that you will be able to stand firm against all strategies and tricks of the Devil.

Ephesians 6:11 NLT

176

Grow in grace, and in the knowledge of our Lord and Saviour Jesus Christ. To him be glory both now and for ever. Amen.

2 Peter 3:18 KJV

The righteous man will flourish like the palm tree, He will grow like a cedar in Lebanon.

Psalm 92:12 NASB

This is my prayer: that your love may abound more and more in knowledge and depth of insight, so that you may be able to discern what is best and may be pure and blameless until the day of Christ.

Philippians 1:9-10

DEEP ROOTS

Many people see abundant spring rains as a great blessing to farmers, especially if the rains come after the plants have sprouted and are several inches tall. What they don't realize is that even a short drought can have a devastating effect on a crop of seedlings that has received too much rain.

Why? Because during frequent rains, the young plants are not required to push their roots deeper into the soil in search of water. If a drought occurs later, plants with shallow root systems will quickly die.

We often receive abundance in our lives—rich fellowship, great teaching, thorough "soakings" of spiritual blessings. Yet when stress or tragedy enters our lives, we may find ourselves thinking God has abandoned us or is unfaithful. The fact is, we have allowed the "easiness" of our lives to keep us from pushing our spiritual roots deeper. We have allowed others to spoon-feed us, rather than develop our own deep personal relationship with God through prayer and study of His Word.

Only the deeply rooted are able to endure hard times without wilting. The best advice is to enjoy the "rain" while seeking to grow even closer to Him.

STRENGTH

The LORD *is* my rock, and my fortress, and my deliverer; my God, my strength, in whom I will trust; my buckler, and the horn of my salvation, and my high tower.

Psalm 18:2 KJV

He gives strength to those who are tired and more power to those who are weak.

Isaiah 40:29 NCV

178

My soul melts from heaviness;
Strengthen me according to Your word.

Psalm 119:28 NKJV

I have the strength to face all conditions by the power that Christ gives me.

Philippians 4:13 TEV

IN HIS STRENGTH

Jane awoke dripping with perspiration; her fever had just broken. Her body was aching, and she was completely drained. She could not imagine speaking that night, and yet, what was she to do? She was the only speaker scheduled for the church's adult class. To cancel would not only have created a crisis, but she felt it would also reflect a failure of her own professed faith that God heals and helps. Instead of canceling, she prayed.

Throughout the day, Jane did not improve. Still, mustering all the energy she had, she dressed and drove herself to the meeting. Every five minutes, she found herself thinking, *I cannot do this. Only by God's help will I even make it to the lectern.* Every step, every action, required major effort. She could tell her fever had returned.

Once behind the lectern, however, she found that she had energy to speak a sentence, and then another, and yet another. She spoke with great vitality and clarity of thought for nearly an hour. Upon return home, however, she collapsed into her bed, where she stayed and slept for eighteen hours.

Jane later said, "What I could not possibly have done in my own strength, I did in His strength."

STRENGTH

In returning and rest shall ye be saved; in quietness and in confidence shall be your strength.

Isaiah 30:15 KJV

I pray that out of his glorious riches he may strengthen you with power through his Spirit in your inner being, so that Christ may dwell in your hearts through faith.

Ephesians 3:16-17

180

They that wait upon the Lord shall renew their strength. They shall mount up with wings like eagles; they shall run and not be weary; they shall walk and not faint.

Isaiah 40:31 TLB

The LORD is my light and my salvation; whom shall I fear? the LORD is the strength of my life; of whom shall I be afraid?

Psalm 27:1 KJV

STANDING YOUR GROUND

In the 1960s, drug companies were presenting nearly 700 applications a year to the Federal Drug Administration for new medicines. The beleaguered New Drug Section only had sixty days to review each drug before giving approval or requesting more data.

A few months after Dr. Frances Kelsey joined the FDA, an established pharmaceutical firm in Ohio applied for a license to market a new drug, Kevadon. In liquid form, the drug seemed to relieve nausea in early pregnancy. It was given to millions of expectant women, mostly in Europe, Asia, and Africa. Although scientific studies revealed harmful side effects, the pharmaceutical firm printed 66,957 leaflets declaring its safety. The company exerted great pressure on Dr. Kelsey to give permission for labels to be printed in anticipation of the drug's approval.

Dr. Kelsey reviewed the data and said no. Through several rounds of applications, she continued to find the data "unsatisfactory." After a fourteen-month struggle, the company humbly withdrew its application. "Kevadon" was thalidomide, and by that name, the horror of thalidomide deformities was becoming well publicized! One firm no decision by Dr. Kelsey spared untold agony in the United States.

Sometimes standing your ground on something may not seem that important, but in time you may see the "big" picture.

STRESS

In my distress I cried out to the LORD. . . .
He heard me from his sanctuary; my cry
reached his ears.

2 Samuel 22:7 NLT

Jesus said, "Don't let your hearts be troubled.
Trust in God, and trust in me."

John 14:1 NCV

182

Leave your troubles with the LORD, and he
will defend you; he never lets honest people
be defeated.

Psalm 55:22 TEV

Fear not, for I am with you. Do not be dismayed.
I am your God. I will strengthen you; I will
help you; I will uphold you with my victorious
right hand.

Isaiah 41:10 TLB

THE RIGHT RESULTS

Sadie Delaney's father taught her to try to do better than her competition. Shortly before she received her teaching license, a supervisor came to watch her and two other student teachers. Their assignment was to teach a class to bake cookies. Since the supervisor didn't have time for each student teacher to go through the entire lesson, she assigned a portion of the lesson to each of the student teachers. Sadie was assigned to teach the girls how to serve and clean up.

The first student teacher panicked and forgot to halve the recipe and preheat the oven. The second girl was so behind because of the first girl's errors that the students made a mess in forming and baking the cookies.

Then it was Sadie's turn. She said to the girls, "We'll have to work together as a team." They quickly baked the remaining dough. Several girls scrubbed pans as soon as the cookies came out of the oven. Within ten minutes, they had several dozen perfect cookies and a clean kitchen. The supervisor was so impressed she offered Sadie a substitute teacher's license on the spot.

Do what it takes to get right results. Your leadership will be marked with less stress and more success!

STRESS

In the day of my trouble I will call upon You,
For You will answer me.

Psalm 86:7 NKJV

Let us not become weary in doing good, for at
the proper time we will reap a harvest if we do
not give up.

Galatians 6:9

Consider it all joy, my brethren, when you
encounter various trials, knowing that the testing
of your faith produces endurance.

James 1:2-3 NASB

"Come to me, all of you who are weary and carry
heavy burdens, and I will give you rest."

Matthew 11:28 NLT

184

AN UNRAVELED WITNESS

A minister was scheduled to speak at an all-day conference. He failed to set his alarm, however, and he overslept. In his haste to make up for lost time, he cut himself while shaving. Then when he went to iron his wrinkled shirt, he scorched it because the iron was too hot. To make matters worse, he noticed that he had a flat tire on his car.

By the time the minister finished changing the tire, he was an hour behind schedule. He figured that if he hurried, he might be only a few minutes late for the first session. He raced through town, only to be stopped by a policeman for speeding.

The agitated minister said sharply, "Officer, go ahead and give me a ticket. Everything else has gone wrong today."

The policeman quietly responded, "I used to have stressful days like yours before I became a Christian."

The minister hung his head in shame. He had forgotten to start his day with God and had allowed stress to unravel his Christian witness.

As a Christian, your actions speak louder than your words, so start your day with prayer, and don't let stress damage your Godly witness.

SUCCESS

It is very good if a man has received wealth from the Lord, and the good health to enjoy it. To enjoy your work and to accept your lot in life—that is indeed a gift from God.

Ecclesiastes 5:19 TLB

186

Riches and honor are with me, enduring wealth and prosperity. My fruit is better than gold, even fine gold, and my yield than choice silver.

Proverbs 8:18-19 RSV

The mind of man plans his way,
But the LORD directs his steps.

Proverbs 16:9 NASB

Wealth and riches are in his house, and his righteousness endures forever.

Psalm 112:3

NO "EASY" DEGREE

Many people face the temptation to slack off once they have achieved a goal. At that point, it's easy to let go of yesterday's insecurities and insufficiencies and accept the illusion that one has arrived.

Professional athletes are especially aware of the danger of such complacency. Even while competing at their peak performance, they face the challenge of preparing themselves for the time when their skills fade and the adulation ends. Those who don't prepare, often settle into marginal careers, and some hit bottom.

In the 1960s, Dave Bing was the NBA's leading scorer in his second year as a Detroit Piston. Today, he is still considered one of basketball's greatest players. Bing thought ahead. Before he went pro, he attended Syracuse University. His advisors suggested he skip the serious courses and earn an "easy" degree. Bing refused, and he took tough business classes instead.

During his pro years, he continued his education, reading voraciously on road trips and taking off-season jobs at a bank, a steel mill, and the Chrysler Corporation. Today, he is the CEO of three multi-million-dollar companies that employ more than 300 people, and he is one of the most successful black businessmen in the nation.

Don't let one success keep you from pressing on to bigger and better things. Constantly set new goals, and you will attain things you never dreamed were possible.

SUCCESS

"I know the plans I have for you," declares the
LORD, "plans to prosper you and not to harm you,
plans to give you hope and a future."
Jeremiah 29:11

True humility and respect for the Lord lead a
man to riches, honor and long life.
Proverbs 22:4 TLB

They are like trees growing beside a stream, trees
that produce fruit in season and always have leaves.
Those people succeed in everything they do.
Psalm 1:3 CEV

The LORD your God will make you most
prosperous in all the work of your hands and in the
fruit of your womb, the young of your livestock
and the crops of your land.
Deuteronomy 30:9

188

HARD WORK

Juan grew up in Puerto Rico, the son of a sugar-cane plantation foreman. He lived with his family of eight in a three-room shack with a dirt floor and no toilet. His first job, at the age of six, was to drive oxen to plow the cane fields eight hours a day for one dollar, with no breaks.

It was in the cane fields that he learned to be on time, work hard, and be loyal and respectful to his employers. At age seven, he got a job at a golf course spotting balls for golfers.

Juan began to dream of playing golf. He made a club out of a guava limb and a piece of pipe, and then he hammered an empty tin can into a ball. Next, he dug two small holes in the ground and hit the ball back and forth between them. He practiced "golf" with the same intensity he had put into his job in the cane field, only this time he was driving golf balls with a club, rather than oxen with a stick. Over time, he became a very good golfer.

In his thirty-one years as a pro golfer, Juan "Chi Chi" Rodriguez has won twenty-four tournaments and earned four million dollars.

No matter how or where you started out in life, you can use your circumstances for your benefit, if you keep the right attitude.

SWEARING

Keep your tongue from evil and your lips from speaking lies.

Psalm 34:13

Let no corrupt word proceed out of your mouth, but what is good for necessary edification, that it may impart grace to the hearers.

Ephesians 4:29 NKJV

190

"I tell you this, that you must give an account on judgment day of every idle word you speak."

Matthew 12:36 NLT

I will watch my ways and keep my tongue from sin; I will put a muzzle on my mouth.

Psalm 39:1

YOUR CALLING CARD

The oldest sister of Daniel Webster married a man named John Colby, the most wicked, Godless man in his neighborhood when it came to swearing and impiety. Then news came to Webster that there was a change in Colby. He decided to call on him to see if it was true.

Upon entering his sister's home, he noticed a large Bible opened on a table. Colby had been reading it prior to his arrival. Colby immediately asked him, "Are you a Christian?" When he was assured of Webster's faith, he suggested that they kneel together and pray.

After the visit, Daniel Webster told a friend, "I would like to hear what enemies of religion say of Colby's conversion. Here was a man as unlikely to be a Christian as any I ever saw; he had gone his Godless way until now, with old age and habits hard to change! Yet to see him a penitent, trusting, humble believer! That is nothing short of the grace of Almighty God."

The fruit of your faith is always found in your words and deeds. You cannot hide what you believe, for your words are your calling card. They will always give away the secrets of your heart.

SWEARING

If you claim to be religious but don't control your tongue, you are just fooling yourself, and your religion is worthless.

James 1:26 NLT

He who guards his lips guards his life, but he who speaks rashly will come to ruin.

Proverbs 13:3

Let every man be swift to hear, slow to speak, slow to wrath.

James 1:19 KJV

There must be no filthiness and silly talk, or coarse jesting, which are not fitting, but rather giving of thanks.

Ephesians 5:4 NASB

WORDS CAN MAKE A DIFFERENCE

Two farmers lived next to each other, with nothing but a river dividing their properties. One day, the cows of one neighbor crossed the river into the other farmer's field of corn. They trampled and ruined about half an acre of the crop. The farmer who owned the damaged corn crop rounded up the cattle. He angrily cursed his neighbor, and before he would return the cows to him, he made him pay dearly for every ear of corn they had destroyed.

Later that fall, the angry farmer awoke to find his hogs across the river. By the time he rounded up his wayward hogs, they had obliterated an entire potato patch. The angry farmer readied himself for a confrontation with the other farmer. But when he saw that his neighbor had no intention of hurling curses or exacting retribution, he was surprised. He said to him, "I cursed you for the damage your cows did, yet you said nothing about my hogs. Why is that?"

The neighbor replied, "Because I am a Christian."

Because of the words he did *not* say, the Christian farmer had the opportunity to witness to his neighbor, and as a result, the angry farmer was converted that very night.

As a leader, you must choose your words carefully, and remember, often times your silence is more effective than a barrage of words!

TEMPTATION

God is never tempted to do wrong, and he never tempts anyone else either.

James 1:13 NLT

194

We do not have a High Priest who cannot sympathize with our weaknesses, but was in all *points* tempted as *we are, yet* without sin. Let us therefore come boldly to the throne of grace, that we may obtain mercy and find grace to help in time of need.

Hebrews 4:15-16 NKJV

Use every piece of God's armor to resist the enemy whenever he attacks, and when it is all over, you will still be standing up.

Ephesians 6:13 TLB

Submit yourselves to God. Resist the Devil, and he will run away from you.

James 4:7 TEV

THE FLAME OF FAITH

The son of a sea captain was confirmed one Sunday morning. Later that day in his cabin, the skipper was anxious to stress the importance of the service that his son had experienced that morning. He said to him, "Son, light this candle, go out on the deck, and return to the cabin with the candle burning."

"But, Father," the boy protested, "if I go on the deck, the wind will surely blow it out."

"Go," the captain said. "Do it."

So the son went. With much shielding and maneuvering, he managed to keep the flame burning. With a sense of relief and accomplishment, he returned to the cabin and showed the candle to his father.

His father then said to him, "Son, you were confirmed today. Your faith is still small. Yet you are growing up and are about to enter the big, tempting world that will do its best to snuff out the flame of your faith. You must keep it properly shielded." It was a vivid lesson the boy never forgot.

Temptation comes to everyone. It must be carefully avoided and consistently refused so that the flame of faith will neither flicker nor die.

TEMPTATION

If sinners entice you, turn your back on them!
Proverbs 1:10 NLT

No temptation has overtaken you but such as is
common to man; and God is faithful, who will not
allow you to be tempted beyond what you are able,
but with the temptation will provide the way of
escape also, so that you may be able to endure it.
1 Corinthians 10:13 NASB

People are tempted when their own evil desire
leads them away and traps them.
James 1:14 NCV

The Lord knoweth how to deliver the godly out
of temptations.
2 Peter 2:9 KJV

196

A NEEDED ADJUSTMENT

A woman was working on her taxes one night when she made an unpleasant discovery. She noticed that her income from the previous year was higher than she had thought, so she owed more taxes than she had anticipated. Her son suggested she just "adjust" the figures. "I can't do that," she replied. "That would be lying."

Yet even as she spoke, the woman realized that she had already given in to the same temptation at work. At the bank where she worked, her boss had often asked her to change dates, add signatures, or "adjust" figures. That night she realized she could no longer participate in the deceit.

The next time her boss asked her to "help out," she refused. A few weeks later, the vice president of the bank asked the woman if she had altered any documents. She admitted that she had and was then told that others in the organization had been put in the same position. She and several other employees met with the board of directors, the truth came out, and her boss was fired.

Nobody can rob you of your integrity. You alone have the power to diminish or destroy it by the way you handle temptation.

THANKFULNESS

Let your roots grow down into him and draw up
nourishment from him. See that you go on
growing in the Lord, and become strong and
vigorous in the truth you were taught. Let your
lives overflow with joy and thanksgiving for all
he has done.

Colossians 2:7 TLB

198

Whatever you do or say, let it be as a
representative of the Lord Jesus, and come with
him into the presence of God the Father to give
him your thanks.

Colossians 3:17 TLB

Thanks be to God, who gives us the victory
through our Lord Jesus Christ.

1 Corinthians 15:57 NASB

Give thanks in all circumstances, for this is God's
will for you in Christ Jesus.

1 Thessalonians 5:18

AN ATTITUDE OF GRATITUDE

Fulton Oursler told a story of an old nurse who was born a slave on the eastern shore of Maryland. She had not only attended Fulton's birth but also that of his mother. He credits her for teaching him the greatest lesson he ever learned about thankfulness and contentment. Recalls Oursler:

> I remember her as she sat at the kitchen table in our house—the hard, old, brown hands folded across her starched apron; the glistening eyes; and the husky old whispering voice, saying, "Much obliged, Lord, for my vittles."
>
> "Anna," I asked, "what's a vittle?"
>
> "It's what I've got to eat and drink—that's vittles," the old nurse replied.
>
> "But you'd get your vittles whether you thanked the Lord or not."
>
> "Sure," said Anna, "but it makes everything taste better to be thankful."

For many people, poverty is not a condition of the pocketbook but a state of mind. Do you think of yourself as being rich or poor today? What do you value and count as "wealth" in your life? If you are thankful for what you have, you are very wealthy indeed!

THANKFULNESS

Give thanks to the LORD, for he is good; his love endures forever. . . . Let them give thanks to the LORD for his unfailing love and his wonderful deeds for men. Let them sacrifice thank offerings and tell of his works with songs of joy.

Psalm 107:1,21-22

200

The LORD is my strength and my shield; my heart trusts in him, and I am helped. My heart leaps for joy and I will give thanks to him in song.

Psalm 28:7

He turned my sorrow into joy! He took away my clothes of mourning and clothed me with joy so that I might sing glad praises to the Lord. . . . O Lord my God, I will keep on thanking you forever!

Psalm 30:11-12 TLB

O come, let us sing for joy to the LORD;
Let us shout joyfully to the rock of our salvation.
Let us come before His presence with thanksgiving,
Let us shout joyfully to Him with psalms.

Psalm 95:1-2 NASB

THOU SHALT NOT WHINE

Here are four steps for turning whining into thanksgiving:

1. *Give something away.* When you give, you create both a physical and a mental space for something new and better to come into your life. Although you may think you are "lacking" something in life, when you give, you demonstrate the abundance you have.

2. *Narrow your goals.* Don't expect everything good to come into your life all at once. When you focus your expectations toward specific, attainable goals, you are more apt to direct your time and energy toward reaching them.

3. *Change your vocabulary from "I need" to "I want."* Most of the things we think we need are actually things we want. If you change your thinking, you will be thankful for even small luxuries that you receive, rather than seeing them as necessities you can't live without.

4. *Choose to be thankful for what you already have.* Thanksgiving is a choice. We all have more things to be thankful for than we could even begin to recount in a single day.

As you put these steps into practice, you will find yourself whining less and thanking God more. You will discover that living a life of gratitude and thanksgiving to God is the perfect antidote for stress!

TRUTH

Surely you heard of him and were taught in him
in accordance with the truth that is in Jesus.
Ephesians 4:21

All Scripture is inspired by God and is useful for
teaching the truth, rebuking error, correcting
faults, and giving instruction for right living.
2 Timothy 3:16 TEV

The words of the LORD are flawless, like silver
refined in a furnace of clay, purified seven times.
Psalm 12:6

The LORD hates . . . A proud look, A lying
tongue, Hands that shed innocent blood.
Proverbs 6:16–17 NKJV

SPEAKING THE TRUTH IN LOVE

Peter Cartwright was a nineteenth-century circuit-riding Methodist preacher. He had a reputation for being a hard preacher and an uncompromising man.

One Sunday morning as he was about to take the pulpit, he was told that President Andrew Jackson was in the congregation. He was warned not to say anything out of line, anything that might be controversial to the president.

Cartwright stood to preach and immediately announced, "I understand that Andrew Jackson is here. I have been requested to be guarded in my remarks. Andrew Jackson will go to hell if he doesn't repent."

The congregation was shocked. They sat in stunned silence, wondering how the president might respond. Jackson didn't flinch.

After the service, President Jackson sought out Peter Cartwright to shake his hand. He said, "Sir, if I had a regiment of men like you, I could whip the world."

Speaking the truth is not an excuse for making hurtful comments or rendering unwanted advice, but there are times when the truth will be compromised if you fail to speak up. Consider first your own motives and then speak the truth in love. Have the courage of your convictions. When coupled with the proper attitude, the truth will always make a positive difference in the lives of others and your own life as well.

TRUTH

Do not testify falsely against your neighbor.
Exodus 20:16 NLT

We will lovingly follow the truth at all times—
speaking truly, dealing truly, living truly—and so
become more and more in every way like Christ.
Ephesians 4:15–16 TLB

204

[Jesus said]: "This is why I was born and came into
the world: to tell people the truth. And everyone
who belongs to the truth listens to me."
John 18:37 NCV

Now, O LORD GOD, You are God, and
Your words are truth.
2 Samuel 7:28 NASB

FESSIN' UP

Bill Campbell, owner of Campbell's Restaurant Equipment & Supply in San Luis Obispo, California, was surprised to find a $10 bill in his mail one day. It was from a customer who had purchased a refrigerator from his company in 1963.

The note attached to the bill read: "I was undercharged $10. When the salesman called to inform me, I refused to pay the $10. I have suffered with this all these years. So here's the $10. Thanks."

Campbell, whose father started the business in 1939, only vaguely remembers hearing about an irate customer who was undercharged and refused to pay. The details are fuzzy in his memory, and he said about the incident, "That was $10 we wrote off."

To Campbell, the $10 bill is too valuable to put in the bank. It's more important to him as a conversation piece, framed and hanging on his wall. Campbell wishes, however, that the customer would have given his name or a return address. "He needs a word of thanks," says Campbell. "He did fess up to it."

WISDOM

To be wise, you must have reverence for the Lord.
Job 28:28 TEV

If any of you needs wisdom, you should ask God
for it. He is generous and enjoys giving to all
people, so he will give you wisdom.
James 1:5 NCV

206

I will instruct you and teach you in the way you
should go; I will counsel you and watch over you.
Psalm 32:8

Determination to be wise is the first step toward
becoming wise! And with your wisdom, develop
common sense and good judgment.
Proverbs 4:7 TLB

THE MISSING SHOVEL

In *Miracle on the River Kwai,* Ernest Gordon tells how Scottish soldiers were forced by their Japanese captors to work on a jungle railroad. They worked in deplorable conditions under barbarous guards.

One day, the officer in charge became enraged over a missing shovel. He pulled his gun and promised to kill all the men unless the guilty party stepped forward. After several tense moments, a man finally stepped out of the line. The officer put his gun away, picked up the shovel, and beat the man to death right in front of the other prisoners. They were allowed only to pick up his bloody corpse and carry it with them to a second tool check. There, the tools were recounted, and all shovels were accounted for—there had never been a missing shovel. There had simply been a miscount at the first checkpoint.

Word of the incident quickly spread through the entire prison camp. An innocent man had been willing to die to save the others. The incident had a profound effect, binding the prisoners together in deep loyalty. It was that loyalty, in part, that gave the men strength to survive until they were liberated.

A wise leader realizes that personal sacrifice is often necessary to inspire others. It brings hope and encouragement to weary souls. It produces growth and maturity. There is no true leadership without some kind of sacrifice.

WISDOM

I guide you in the way of wisdom and lead you along straight paths. When you walk, your steps will not be hampered; when you run, you will not stumble.

Proverbs 4:11-12

The Lord grants wisdom! His every word is a treasure of knowledge and understanding.

Proverbs 2:6 TLB

Your commands make me wiser than my enemies, because they are mine forever. I am wiser than all my teachers, because I think about your rules.

Psalm 119:98-99 NCV

What seems to be God's foolishness is wiser than human wisdom, and what seems to be God's weakness is stronger than human strength.

1 Corinthians 1:25 TEV

SIMPLE SOLUTIONS

After Thomas Edison's fame had become international, he was advised to have scientists come to his lab and help him understand just why some of his inventions had worked. Edison didn't see much use for it, but being open-minded, he consented to the idea. As a result, a brilliant research scientist from Germany came to his lab to explain to him the principles behind some of his innovations.

Edison handed the man a globe that had been twisted into a gourd-like shape and said, "Give me the cubic content of this."

Weeks passed, and eventually Edison sought out the man to ask him why he hadn't replied. The scientist began to give him a lengthy explanation about the difficulties of solving such a problem with higher mathematics. Edison then picked up the globe, took it over to a nearby sink, and filled it with water. He poured the water into a measuring tube, and holding up the tube he said, "This is the cubic content."

The solutions to most problems are probably far simpler than we think they might be. They usually stem from an understanding of basic principles, the whys of life. Ask God to give you wisdom so that you will be able to discover the simple solutions to your problems.

WITNESS

"Go, then, to all peoples everywhere and make them my disciples: baptize them in the name of the Father, the Son, and the Holy Spirit, and teach them to obey everything I have commanded you."

Matthew 28:19-20 TEV

"When the Holy Spirit has come upon you, you will receive power to testify about me with great effect."

Acts 1:8 TLB

The followers went everywhere in the world and told the Good News to people, and the Lord helped them. The Lord proved that the Good News they told was true by giving them power to work miracles.

Mark 16:20 NCV

"You are my witnesses," declares the LORD, "that I am God."

Isaiah 43:12

WHAT'S YOUR MISSION?

A businessman once saw a man carrying a backpack with a well-worn sign that read, "I will work for food." Although the businessman didn't usually respond to such pleas, this time he did. He invited the backpacker to lunch, and in the course of their conversation, discovered that the man was not homeless but on a mission.

The backpacker admitted that he had seen rough times early in his life, had made some wrong choices, and had paid the consequences. But fourteen years earlier, while backpacking across the country, he had given his life to God. Ever since, he had felt God calling him to work to buy food and Bibles. Then, whenever he felt led, he would give the Bibles away.

His backpack was already filled with Bibles, but when the businessman asked him if he could use one more, the backpacker readily accepted. In return, he gave his benefactor his well-worn work gloves and asked, "Whenever you see these gloves, will you pray for me?"

The businessman replied, "You bet." These gloves still sit on his desk today, reminding him to pray.

The Lord has a ministry designed to fit the unique qualities He has built into each one of us. Have you found and accepted your specific mission?

WITNESS

"You are My witnesses," says the LORD,
"And My servant whom I have chosen,
That you may know and believe Me,
And understand that I am He.
Before Me there was no God formed,
Nor shall there be after Me."

Isaiah 43:10 NKJV

212

He said to them, "Go into all the world and preach
the gospel to every creature."

Mark 16:15 NKJV

"Repentance for forgiveness of sins would be
proclaimed in His name to all the nations,
beginning from Jerusalem."

Luke 24:47 NASB

They that were scattered abroad went every
where preaching the word.

Acts 8:4 KJV

SING HIS PRAISE

Voltaire said that he would destroy, within just a few years, what it took Christ eighteen centuries to establish. He hoped to replace what he perceived as a faulty philosophy with a better one of his own creation. However, Voltaire's words were to become only hollow bragging. His own printing press was later used to print Bibles, and his log cabin became a storage place for them.

Reformation leader Martin Luther once said, "I pray you leave my name alone. Do not call yourselves Lutherans, but Christians." John Wesley expressed a similar sentiment when he said, "I wish the name Methodist might never be mentioned again, but lost in eternal oblivion." Charles Spurgeon said, "I look forward with pleasure to the day when there will not be a Baptist living. I say of the Baptist name, let it perish, but let Christ's own name last forever."

We err anytime we seek to sing our own praises. For the Christian, the only One truly worthy to be praised is the Lord God. Rather than exalting yourself today, seek to exalt the One whose name will last forever and before whom every knee will one day bow. Let your witness for the Lord ring clear and true, unencumbered by any name but His.

WORK

Work hard and cheerfully at all you do, just as though you were working for the Lord and not merely for your masters, remembering that it is the Lord Christ who is going to pay you, giving you your full portion of all he owns. He is the one you are really working for.

Colossians 3:23-24 TLB

When God gives any man wealth and possessions, and enables him to enjoy them, to accept his lot and be happy in his work—this is a gift of God.

Ecclesiastes 5:19

"Don't work for food that spoils. Work for food that gives eternal life. The Son of Man will give you this food, because God the Father has given him the right to do so."

John 6:27 CEV

God is not unfair. He will not forget how hard you have worked for him and how you have shown your love to him by caring for other Christians, as you still do.

Hebrews 6:10 NLT

WORK SHOULD BE FUN

Professor Basil L. Gildersleeve of Johns Hopkins University was once interviewed for the *Saturday Evening Post*. At the time, the elderly professor was considered the greatest Greek scholar in the nation, and his work had been honored by numerous organizations and societies around the world.

The interviewer asked Professor Gildersleeve what he considered to be the highest award or compliment he had ever received. He thought for a moment and then replied, "I believe it was when one of my students said, 'Professor, you have so much fun with your own mind!'"

Behavioral researchers have discovered that when people enjoy their work and feel it is meaningful, they are more productive, more open to improvement, and more concerned about the quality of their work. As their levels of productivity and quality rise, they become more efficient and actually begin to earn more money—either through promotions, pay raises, or a broader customer base. As their income increases, they tend to enjoy their work even more!

To be a truly effective leader, you must find pleasure in your work. Find something you sincerely enjoy doing, then do it well. Success will surely follow!

WORK

Six days shall work be done: but the seventh day is
the sabbath of rest, an holy convocation; ye shall
do no work therein: it is the sabbath of the LORD
in all your dwellings.

Leviticus 23:3 KJV

Each man's work will become evident; for the
day will show it because it is to be revealed with
fire, and the fire itself will test the quality of each
man's work.

1 Corinthians 3:13 NASB

God has promised us a Sabbath when we will rest,
even though it has not yet come. On that day
God's people will rest from their work, just as
God rested from his work.

Hebrews 4:9-10 CEV

Even when we were with you, we gave you this
rule: "If a man will not work, he shall not eat."

2 Thessalonians 3:10

THE GIFT OF SERVICE

Shortly after Booker T. Washington became head of the Tuskegee Institute in Alabama, he was walking past the house of a wealthy family. The woman of the house, assuming Washington was one of the yard workers her husband had hired, asked him if he would chop some wood for her. Professor Washington smiled, nodded, took off his coat, and chopped the wood. When he carried the armload of wood into the woman's kitchen, a servant girl recognized him and rushed to her mistress to tell her of his identity.

The next morning, the woman appeared in Washington's office. Apologizing profusely, she said repeatedly, "I did not know it was you I put to work."

Washington replied with generosity, "It's entirely all right, madam. I like to work, and I'm delighted to do favors for my friends."

The woman was so taken with his manner and his willingness to forgive that she gave generous gifts to the institute and persuaded many of her wealthy acquaintances to do likewise. In the end, Washington raised as much money for the institute from this one act of chopping wood as he did from any other fund-raising event!

A great leader is never beyond hard work. The willingness to serve others is the essence of true leadership.

WORRY

Don't worry about anything; instead, pray about everything; tell God your needs and don't forget to thank him for his answers.

Philippians 4:6 TLB

"Do not worry about tomorrow; it will have enough worries of its own. There is no need to add to the troubles each day brings."

Matthew 6:34 TEV

Give all your worries and cares to God, for he cares about what happens to you.

1 Peter 5:7 NLT

You will keep him in perfect peace, Whose mind is stayed on You, Because he trusts in You.

Isaiah 26:3 NKJV

BON APPÉTIT

n *Living, Loving and Learning,* Leo Buscaglia
writes:

I always talk about Julia Child. I really like
her attitude. She's someone I would write to. I
watch her because she does such wonderful
things: "Tonight we're going to make a
soufflé." And she beats this and she whisks
that, and she throws things on the floor. She
wipes her face in her napkin and she does all
these wonderful human things. Then she takes
this soufflé and throws it in the oven, and talks
to you a while. Then says, "Now there's one
ready." When she opens it up, it caves in. You
know what she does? She doesn't kill herself.
She doesn't commit hari-kari with her butcher
knife. She says, "Well, you can't win 'em all.
Bon appétit!" I love it! That's the way we have
to lead our lives. You can't win 'em all. But I
know people who are still flagellating
themselves over mistakes they made twenty
years ago. "I should have done this," and "I
should have done that." Well, it's tough that
you didn't. But who knows what surprises
there are in tomorrow? Learn to say "Bon
appétit." Nobody said you were perfect. It
might even be more interesting. You burned
the dinner, so you go out.[10]

ENDNOTES

[1] (p. 37) *Fortune* (May 1, 1995) p. 32.

[2] (p. 49) Edith Schaeffer, *What Is a Family?* (Ada, MI: Fleming H. Revell Co., 1975) p. 149.

[3] (p. 61) Lloyd John Ogilvie, *Let God Love You* (Dallas, TX: Word, 1974) pp. 139-140.

[4] (p. 77) Catherine Marshall, *A Closer Walk* (Ada, MI: Fleming H. Revell Co., 1986) pp. 102-103.

[5] (p. 91) Robert J. Duncan, *McKinney Living* (McKinney, TX: self-published, 1982) p. 82.

[6] (p. 121) Steven Carter and Julia Sokol, *Lives Without Balance* (New York, NY: Villard Books, Random House, Inc., 1991) pp. 125,194.

[7] (p. 131) *Decision* (September 1994) p. 6.

[8] (p. 139) Catherine Marshall, *A Closer Walk* (Ada, MI: Fleming H. Revell Co., 1986) pp. 102-103.

[9] (p. 153) *1100 Illustrations from the Writings of D. L. Moody,* John Reed, editor (Grand Rapids, MI: Baker Book House, 1996) p. 247.

[10] (p. 219) Leo Buscaglia, *Living, Loving and Learning,* Steven Short, editor (New York, NY: Holt, Rinehart & Winston, 1982) p. 260.